MW01282237

Sitges Travel Guide, Spain

Subtitle to be here

Author
Ibrahim Lloyd.

Publisher:
SONITTEC LTD
College House, 2nd
Floor
17 King Edwards
Road,
Ruislip
London
HA4 7AE

Table of Content

Summary

Wonderful Benefits of Traveling
If there was one piece of advice I have for people today to experience more joy in life, it is to travel more. I don't mean taking vacations or going on pre-planning trips, I mean making the journey out to somewhere you've never gone before with an open schedule, to let life show you what opportunities were waiting for you that you couldn't have even imaged before.

Traveling is wonderful in many ways. It captures us with a sense of wanderlust and has us longing for more destinations to visit, cultures to experience, food to eat, and people to meet. As amazing as traveling is, most of us think we need to wait until our later years to really explore a lot of the world. I want to inspire you to travel more now and I will do that by sharing 9 wonderful benefits of traveling so you can take the leap of faith you've been waiting for.

You'll find a new purpose

To travel is to take a journey into yourself.

Traveling is an amazingly underrated investment in yourself. As you travel you're exposed to more new people, cultures, and lifestyles than you are living in your homeland all the time. With all the newness in your life, you're also opened to new insights, ways of seeing the world and living, which often gives people a new purpose for their lives. If you're feeling stuck on what your purpose is, what you want to do with your life, the career or educational path you want to pursue, go travel...you might just be surprised about what you discover as a new sense of life purpose and direction.

You'll appreciate your home more

All travel has it's advantages. If the passenger visits better countries, he may learn to improve his own. And if fortune carries him to worse, he may learn to enjoy it.

When we spend time away from home, especially in a place where we don't have the same luxuries readily available to us...like a village in Fiji that runs without electricity...we become more aware and appreciative for the luxuries we have back at home. I remember a time where I visited my cousin in Argentina after she'd been living there for about a year. I was visiting her around Christmas time and brought her the new Harry Potter book along with some basic goods that you can find almost anywhere in

Los Angeles. She was over joyous and filled with gratitude, like she just got the greatest gift in the world. In other parts of the world, like India and Ethiopia, people don't have as much access to clean drinking water...especially from what's readily available on tap. Traveling through areas like that really make us appreciate what we do have, and often can spark the movement of something to support people living there experience a greater quality of life.

You'll realize that your home is more than just where you grew up

No one realizes how beautiful it is to travel until he comes home and rests his head on his old, familiar pillow.

The more we travel, the more we realize that our home is so much more than the town, city, state and even country that we've grown up in; we realize that our home is the world, this planet, and we become more conscious of how we can harmoniously live and support one another. And in that knowingness and state of consciousness, people like those supporting the movement of charity:water come into fruition.

You'll realize how little you actually knew about the world

The world is a book, and those who do not travel read only one page

There's concept, and then there's experience. When we travel, we may notice that some of the things we've heard about the world end up being very different than what we were indoctrinated and conditioned to believe. Many of the initial myths that get dispelled are often about traveling itself. Where you once may have thought it was too expensive and dangerous, you may realize how you can actually save more on your lifestyle expenses traveling the world than you do living at home. You may also realize how kind and friendly strangers can be, and how they are even willing to take care of you with a place to sleep at night. Beyond that, you have the whole world to learn about with every place you discover, every person you meet and every culture you experience.

You'll realize that we all share similar needs
Travel is fatal to prejudice, bigotry, and narrow-mindedness.
Tony Robbins has said many times that no matter what your background is, all human beings share 6 common needs. As you travel more, you notice the truth of this even more…and as that happens, you are more adept in being able to relate to people regardless of their background.

You'll realize that it's extremely easy to make friends

A journey is best measured in friends, rather than miles.

One of the first things I learned from traveling solo is how easy it is to make friends. Something magical happens in how people can show up more raw and real when they're out of their conditioned environment and open to express themselves without feeling judged. That rawness and realness ends up inspiring others to be authentic, and that's how you can become best friends with people when you've only known them for a few hours.

You'll experience the interconnectedness of humanity

Perhaps travel cannot prevent bigotry, but by demonstrating all peoples cry, laugh, eat, worry, and die, it can introduce the idea that if we try and understand each other, we may even become friends.

Just as we notice how we share similar needs, how our perspective of our home expands, and how we become close friends with others from different backgrounds and cultures, we begin to realize how we are all connected. This state of awareness is a jump in consciousness, and what I mean by that is in the way we perceive the world, the life experience and ourselves. Ken Wilber speaks about consciousness as spiral dynamics, each level of consciousness inclusive of the one previous. I feel that traveling often helps people experience a world-centric view of consciousness, and some even on that's integrated...able to see, understand and accept all states of consciousness, and utilizing the gifts of whatever is best and most appropriate in the moment.

You'll experience serendipity and synchronicity

Traveling is one of the easiest ways to become aware of the magic that weaves all of creation together through serendipity and synchronicity with perfect timing.

Serendipity: luck that takes the form of finding valuable or pleasant things that are not looked for. And here's Synchronicity: coincidence of events that appear meaningfully related but do not seem to be causally connected

I'm going to share one story of how I experienced serendipity and synchronicity in Spain. It was early in the morning and it was time for me to return the motorcycle my friend had rented with me yesterday. She left very early in the morning on a flight home so it was my responsibility to return it. I woke up to a beautiful sunny morning in Spain and went out to the street to start the motorcycle. I started to drive, forgetting that the chain was left on the wheel. Having no previous experience with motorcycles, I realized I was in a predicament. Two minutes later, a car drove and parked behind me. I had a feeling that someone in that vehicle knew how to fix motorcycles and was going to help me remove the chain so I could return the motorcycle. As they got out, I spoke to them in Spanish, telling them what happened. One of them motioned the other to go on. He mentioned they were mechanics and here for a job, and that he could help me get the chain off…and he did. I thanked him and he seemed gratified to help a fellow soul on their way. In that moment, I realized that no matter what…the world is here to support me, which leads us to the last benefit of traveling.

You'll realize life is a wonderful gift
Life is either a daring adventure or nothing.

"Twenty years from now you will be more disappointed by the things that you didn't do than by the ones you did do. So throw off the bowlines. Sail away from the safe harbor. Catch the trade winds in your sails. Explore. Dream. Discover." Mark Twain

Life is a wonderful gift. It really is, and as we travel and experience more of the world and life, we often become overwhelmed with gratitude and appreciation for all the beautiful moments we enjoyed and people we've shared them with. More often than not, this is a realization that we can experience and take action from now while we're still alive with energy rather than stacking up regrets by the time we're on our death bed. Rather than waiting until you're saying "I wish I had", live so you can say "I'm glad I did".

Introduction

All the information you need about Sitges. Not only for residents but also for casual visitors, Tourists, people interested in moving to Sitges, residents of surrounding towns or indeed anyone with an interest in Sitges. Information covers cultural activities, festivals, social activities, bureaucratic procedures, schooling, leisure activities, associations, special offers, transport, shops, parking and a large etc. This book offers information and answers to all issues that may arise when living, visiting or planning to live in Sitges - all on one book.

Sitges is a Mediterranean coastal town, located in the Garraf area in the province of Barcelona, in Catalonia, Spain. Sheltered by the Garraf mountains and due to its geographical position in the Mediterranean, Sitges has a warm "micro-climate" that makes it possible to enjoy outdoor activities almost every day of the year. Moreover, throughout the year numerous events take place in this beautiful town: the Sitges International Fantastic Film Festival of Catalonia, Carnival, the Festa Major, Theatre Festivals, The Barcelona-Sitges Vintage Car Rally, Harvest Festival, concerts ... the list goes on, however one can also enjoy simply taking a stroll along the sea-front boulevard, a bike ride through the Garraf Natural Park or soak up the atmosphere of the Sitges nights on the renowned "Dos de Mayo" street.

Four kilometres of beach with a delightful sea-front promenade featuring turn of the 20th century colonial "Indiano" mansions on one side and the sea on the other, makes it always a good excuse for a trip to Sitges.

Sitges with its year-round mild climate and coastal location offers a wide range of sports and water-sport activities. Numerous sports events are held throughout the year such as the Mitja Sitges (Half Marathon), the annual Triathlon, Beach Rugby 7, sailing regattas, 3x3 basketball and football tournaments.

Cultural events always highlight the Sitges calendar throughout the year and include theatre festivals, the International Film Festival, renowned art exhibitions, Carnival, Sitgestiu Cultural organized by Museus de Sitges with daily events during the three summer months, classical and contemporary music concerts, international events such as the Patchwork meet, the vintage Barcelona-Sitges Car Rally or our local fiesta mayor with its exceptional firework display that draws thousands of spectators to the beaches to watch. The list goes on!

Family-friendly Sitges also offers play areas for children such as the large shady Terramar Park with picnic areas and swings, the sandy beaches, the waterfront promenade ideal for roller skating and biking and the local Natural Park of Garraf to enjoy nature. Activities for children include the Christmas Fun Park, the 3 Kings procession of Epiphany, the Junior Carnival with elaborate floats and costumes, the junior parades during the fiesta Mayor and fiesta of Santa Tecla, the Sitges has Talent competition, the junior triathlon and family workshops organized by Museus de Sitges. Sports activities for children are numerous and include sailing, surfing, or joining the many local sports clubs, which include football, rugby, basketball, triathlon and competitive swimming.

Sitges has always been characterized by its tolerance, both of the locals and open-mindedness of visitors too. It's definitely a convivial village where all people are welcome regardless of colour, religion or sexual orientation

History

From the Beginning to 1700

It is known of the first settlers of Sitges, who were nomadic groups that lived on hunting and fishing. The Neanderthal mandible from the Cova del Gegant that was found in the 50s, is about 53,200 years old (one of the oldest human remains in Catalonia).

The archaeological remains found in the vicinity of the Parish and town hall, show that the area was occupied continuously from the sixth century BC to the first century AD. Excavations show that there was a Roman villa in the Vinyet area between the first and third century AD.

The meaning of the name Sitges ("sitja" in Catalan), comes from silos, deep pits in the ground used for grain storage and suggests this could have been an area where these underground silos were frequent.

In the eleventh century AD there was a castle in Sitges however there are no visible remains and its site is where the town hall stands today. Other small castles were built in the same century throughout the territory of Penedés and Garraf and hamlets grew around them in Olivella, Cubelles, La Geltrú and Ribes. The castle of Sitges, the fortified towers & stables of Miralpeix, Campdàsens and Les Botigues de Sitges were under the control of Ribes castle whereas the castle of Garraf was under the rule of

Eramprunyà castle. What is today the municipality of Sitges, was never governed under a single feudal lord.

In the fourteenth century, the "seigneur" of Ribes ceded the castle and domain of Sitges to a family that, two centuries earlier, had adopted the name of the ceded territory. In 1308 Agnés of Sitges sold the rights to Bernat de Fonollar who was lord of the castle until 1326. Bernat of Fonollar was the right-hand man of King James II the Just and became the most important man in the history of medieval Sitges.

Bernat de Fonollar founded the hospital of Sant Joan Baptista in 1324.

He died without heirs (his tomb is at the Altar of the Souls in the parish church) leaving his estate to the Pia Almoina, a charitable institution run by the See of Barcelona. Other lords or "seigneurs" claimed rights over the territories held by Bernat de Fonollar however after litigation the Pia Almoina was recognized as the owner of the castle and the territory of Sitges. The Pia Almoina had to continue to fight lawsuits for another 300 years, brought against them by the "Universitat Sitgetana" (essentially the Sitges town hall which by then already included Garraf, Miralpeix and Campdàsens), who wanted to depend and report directly to the crown.

Sitges lived turbulent times during the seventeenth and eighteenth centuries due to the consequences of war: at the beginning of the conflict between France and Spain (1640-1659), 600 Neapolitan soldiers from Felipe IV of Spain's army overran Sitges and stole everything they could.

In 1649, the town of Sitges came under siege for two days, suffering bombardment by land and sea and looting by the Castilian troops of Juan de Garay (viceroy of Catalonia). This attack caused extensive damage to the town, as well as the collapse of a section of the wall, two towers and part of the castle, which was not to be rebuilt until 1681.

From 1700 to 1900

The War of Succession (1700-1714) also affected the citizens of Sitges; as they continually had to suffer the soldiers on both sides who robbed them, demanded food, shelter...

It was also a time of pirates and bandits (travellers were assaulted on the paths following the coast of Garraf)... however Sitges was able to overcome these hardships and continue to grow.

As a consequence of repeated pirate attacks stone farmhouses, "masias", were fortified and watchtowers added. (See examples of fortified "masias" along the paths in the natural park of Garraf.) A frigate was built as defence against pirates and was moored below "La Punta", a rocky outcrop where the parish church stands today. This area is still known as "La Fragata". The canon currently set into the "Baluard", is a reminder of the six canons that used to be mounted on the bastion, which, in 1797 succeeded in preventing some British frigates from capturing a boat anchored in front of La Punta. The 1778 Free Trade Act with America enabled many Sitges citizens to emigrate to the new continent and conduct import and export business. Those who were successful, upon their return were called "Americanos".

The reconstruction of the parish church of "Sant Bartomeu i Santa Tecla" (known as "La Punta"), replaced the previous building destroyed during the bombing of 1649. The new church was consecrated in 1672 and was completed in 1688, although it wasn't until a century later when the belfry was topped with a statue of the Virgin Mary.

The current Sanctuary of our Lady of Vinyet underwent major reforms between 1727 and 1733. There are documents that date it back to the 12th century and confirm the chapel is located in the same spot, where tradition says an image of the Virgin of Vinyet was found (under a vine, hence the name "Vinyet", typical of Sitges). Two wealthy Sitges families who made their fortune in maritime trade and by reinvesting their profits in land, the Llopis and the Falç families, furthered the urban growth of Sitges with the construction of an "eixample", an extension of the town in a grid fashion, creating the streets of Sant Josep, Sant Bonaventura y Sant Gaudenci (the "Museu Romàntic" also called Casa Llopis) is on Sant Josep.

Wars continued during the nineteenth century (the Peninsula War 1808-1814, the three Carlist wars that ended by 1876...), and despite the unrest Sitges strove to make improvements: the old chapel of San Sebastian was torn down and a new one completed in 1861, improvements were made to the parish church, the porch, an extension, the belfry with the clock from the "Torre de las Hores" destroyed in the 1868 revolution..

Closer ties were forged with the Americas thanks to business, social and cultural relations, especially with Cuba and Puerto Rico.

"Americanos" was the name give to the Sitgetans who returned to Sitges after making their fortune overseas. Around the village there are examples of the beautiful villas that these "americanos" built to prove that they had been successful. They also invested part of their profits in banking, industry, vineyards, recreational societies, and railways... Nowadays, during the Festa Major of Sitges, two of the "gegants" (tall figures with painted papier maché head and arms, and a hollow wooden frame covered in clothing) are endearingly called "los cubanitos" and represent the "americanos" that played such an important role in the development of Sitges. In Santiago de Cuba, Facundo Bacardí founded a company under his name which is known worldwide (Casa Bacardí is a visitors centre housed in the historic Mercat Vell, a Catalan Art Nouveau building in the heart of the old quarter.

The "Unión Suburense", a spinning factory, was the first industry that was set up in Sitges (1847), "els boters" (cask-making or cooperage) was a very profitable business, the recreational society El Retiro was founded in 1870, the oldest one of its kind in Sitges (the headquarters can still be found on the same street)...

The end of the nineteenth century was a time of growth for Sitges, economically, culturally and communication-wise. The "Mercat Vell" (old market) was built, as was the "Ajuntament" (town-hall) and the "Nou Escorxador" (the abbatoir which has since disappeared). Palm trees were planted on the Passeig de la Ribera and Antonio Gaudí built the Celler Güell in Garraf. New industries were set in motion such as shoe manufacturing which was to become the economic motor of the town for many years. A gas factory produced gas for street lamps improving public illumination. Drinking water was piped from Santa Oliva. Access and communication was improved by the opening of the corniche road along the Garraf coast, the building of a railway line that ran between Barcelona and Vilanova i la Geltrú and a telegraph station.

In 1877, the Casino Prado Suburense opened its doors. That same year Sitges' first newspaper, the Revista Suburense, was founded. Another paper, El Eco de Sitges, was published a decade later and is still in print nowadays and there was a third, La Voz de Sitges. Literary contests were held and in 1897 "els gegants de Sitges", the oldest "gegants" in Cataluña were paraded on the streets. Sitges attracted many members of the artistic Luminist school (1880) and among them the most recognised painter at that time, Santiago Rusiñol, an artist of many disciplines and the driving force behind the Festes Modernistes (1892-1899). He left an indelible mark on the Sitges landscape when he acquired two fishermen's houses and converted them into the Cau Ferrat which would serve as both his studio, his home and is now a museum.

The 20th Century

The twentieth century began with the culmination of all the modernization that had taken place towards the end of the previous century. Urban growth continued with the development of the Terramar and Vinyet neighbourhoods, and the Passeig Maritim was built. The staircase from La Fragata to La Punta was completed in 1900, the Cap de la Vila was renovated, large open roads connected the maritime promenade with the Vilanova road and "americanos" built beautiful oceanfront homes some of which are still standing today.

Electricity, the telephone and piped water arrived. The double railroad track between Sitges y Castelldefels was finished. The shoe manufacturing industry initiated at the end of the previous century was consolidated and grew. By 1936, 75% of the Sitges workforce worked in the shoemaking industry. A factory of cement and hydraulic lime mortar was opened in Vallcarca and the corresponding workers colony followed in 1901, housing more than five thousand workers in the mid twentieth century. In the first half of the twentieth century, tourism arrived and the fame of Sitges spread. A tourist information office was set-up, hotels opened (Hotel Subur in 1916, Hotel Terramar in 1933), and cultural facilities were inaugurated (Museu Cau Ferrat and the Santiago Rusiñol library). New schools were opened with such emblematic teachers that some of today's schools in Sitges are named after them: Esteve Barrachina, Maria Ossó, Emili Picó i Magí Casanovas.

The hospital of Sant Joan Baptista was built between 1910 and 1912 and is currently an old people's home. It is a fine example of modernist architecture and the main door and its lantern dome deserve a special mention.

The painter Agustí Ferrer Pino designed the "Drac de Sitges" which was first shown in public at the "Festa Major" in 1922.

The Terramar race-track was the first permanent car-racing circuit in Spain (1923) and the third in Europe.

It was a time when many associations were founded, some of which still continue today: Club

Natació Sitges (swimming club), Club Ciclista Suburense (cycling club), Patronat d'Acció Social Catòlica ...

Sitges was considered a cultured and cosmopolitan town and in its midst lived and worked sculptors, painters, poets, composers and characters as accomplished as Miquel Utrillo (engineer, art critic, cultural organizer...), Joaquim Sunyer (Novecentismo painter) Antoni Català (composer of sacred music and sardanas), Josep Carbonell i Gener (journalist, historian) and Charles Deering (industrialist and North American collector who was so impressed by the beauty of Sitges that he built there the Palau Maricel to house his art collection.

The Spanish Civil War (1936-1939) put a stop to this cultural efflorescence and to Sitges' (and the rest of Catalonia) opening up to the world. A dark period ensued due to the dictatorship, repression, international isolation, social inequalities, and scarcity of raw materials...

From the second half of the twentieth century the situation began to change. Spain joined some international organisations and USA started to support the Franco regime. Tourism started up again and hotels grew threefold. Bars, cafés and nightclubs also experimented an increase in numbers. As tourism bloomed, much of the workforce that had previously been working in shoe manufacturing moved towards jobs in tourism or construction and the shoe industry began to decline. By the seventies, around 75% of the Sitges workforce was working in tourism-related jobs.

As is characteristic of Sitges, the social and cultural life of the village was once again vibrant and all encompassing: in 1970 the Museu Maricel was opened, Artur Carbonell was a great theatre man (and painter) who created many events and variety shows (1906-1973), Pere Jou sculpted the capitals of the Palau Maricel and the friezes of the Casino Prado (1891-1964), Ramon Planas was a great journalist and a prominent intellectual who published novels and essays (1905-1989), Pere Pruna (1904-1977) painted a mural for the baptistery and side chapel in the parish church, the Corpus Christi Festival became an institutionalized event and prizes were awarded to the best flower carpets and best Carnation Display. The first Barcelona to Sitges Vintage Car Rally took place in 1959, the theatre and cinema festivals got going towards the end of the 1960's and the Festa de la Verema (grape harvest festival) became an annual event at the beginning of the 70's.

When Franco's dictatorship ended, there was great political change. The first democratic elections took place in 1979 and Jordi Serra of the political party PSC-PSOE was elected to the town hall. Sitges underwent extraordinary growth that began at the end of the 70's and continues today: with a population of 11,500 registered in 1970, Sitges grew to 28,130 residents in 2010 (municipal census data). This meant the development of new roads and avenues, new residential areas...In 1975 the Port d'Aiguadolç was built. At the beginning of the 90's the C-32 Garraf motorway was opened and its use immediately reduced travel time from Sitges to Barcelona and to the airport. As a result more hotels were built and there was an increased affluence of visitors. Sitges became the second destination in volume for the celebration of congresses in Catalonia.

With the arrival of democracy Sitges was able to reinstate the celebration of Carnival, which had been banned during the dictatorship. With the years the number of floats and participants in the street festivities has grown and the fame of the Sitges Carnival has spread around the world.

Development has not only been at the service of tourism, residents have also benefited with the improvement of parks, services and infrastructures: urban green spaces such as the Terramar gardens or the Hort de Can Falç have been recovered and new parks such as the Parc of Can Robert have been created. New schools have been built, also a new municipal market, a new library and a citizen's advice bureau.

New associations, societies, guilds and clubs were established in the village and they covered all manner of leisure pursuits: culture, sport, and folklore...

The bustling social and cultural lifestyle is written into the DNA of the inhabitants of Sitges. With its white houses, "americano" villas and people greeting each other in the streets (after all Sitges is essentially a small village), it is nevertheless as active culturally as a big city, with film and theatre festivals, a great range of leisure and festive events, Carnival, the Vintage Car Rally, the Menjar de Tast, concerts ... it is difficult to find a weekend where there isn't some sort of celebration, exhibition, parade or public event taking place.

This makes Sitges a unique town that has no use for the word boredom, however having said that it also offers calm spots for those who prefer repose. These contrasts linked with the charm of the locals have made it special: the sea and the mountains of Garraf, its quiet nooks and its streets full of "fiesta", the popular festivities and the International Festivals of Cinema and Theatre, the religious and pagan celebrations...

Tourism

Located on the Mediterranean coast, Sitges has 17 BEACHES that enjoy a mild and temperate climate. It is surrounded by the Garraf's Park mountains, which makes its climate unique. It is over forty-four kilometers squared that are home to twenty-eight thousand inhabitants. In recent years, the number of the inhabitants increased due to the massive immigration of the new, also foreign, inhabitans. Thirty-five percent of its population is composed of foreigners, mainly wealthy families from The Netherlands and United Kingdom, whose children attend international schools nearby.

The city's infrastructure is very tourism oriented. It has three marinas, being the city with most marinas in Spain. During the past years, economic activities have disappeared, giving priority to the tourism market of the region. Besides tourism, some of the economy is based on fishing, due to its geographic location.

As a place that has an old historical background, Sitges still has many historical sites. The most popular one is the Iglesias de Sant Bartomeu I Santa Tecla, the church better known as "La Punta" or "The Tip" for its location on the edge of a coastal hill. It was built in the seventeenth century and carries a mixture of a Baroque and Renaissance style. Hospital de Sant Joan Baptista is another place, worth to visit on your tour around the city. The look at the hospital dated in 14st century definitely fulfill your cultural and historcial needs. The hospital is even listed in the list of the architectural heritage of Catalonia, with a library placed inside currently.

If are you interested in the story and antmosphere of the cemeteries, the cemetery of Sitges will attract you. The graves and mausoelums for the whole families are made with interesting alcoves and sculptures in a modernist architecture from 19th century. The cemetery is listed in the list of architectural heritage of Catalonia as well. On your way of exploring the city, do not miss the Monument a El Greco from the 19th century surrounded by the gardens. It is a stoned sculpture of "El Greco", holding pallete in one hand and a brush in another hand. If you are more museum lover, Maricel Museum or Cau Ferrat Museumin the centre of Sitges are something for you. The expositions contains thousands of items from paintings, Romanesque murals, carvings and atlarpieces to furniture, precious metal, ceramics and porcelain items.

We are bringing you one special tip, that you should not miss on your visit Casa Bacardi Sitges! Maybe you are asking, how is this famous alcohol beverage related to small city such Sitges. The answer is interesting Don Facundo Bacardi, the native from Sitges, emigrated to Cuba and has founded this famous rum company Bacardi in 1862. As a honour to this man, the Museum of Bacardi was built. In the museum, you can learn about the history of family, their life in Cuba and the production of rum. Really unique opportunity is to visit one of their cocktail classes and you will leave with your own made cocktail!

Throughout the years, Sitges hosts many events that attract people from all over the world. The most famous ones are the SITGES FILM FESTIVAL a Catalan film festival that was founded in 1967 and CARNIVAL, the religious holiday that attracts over 250,000 people during its week. Since 2006, also theGAY PRIDE to encourage the rights of LGBT community is organized here.

With large avenues and narrow streets, Sitges is a charming small town. Some streets in the center of the village have exclusive pedestrian and bike access, making a perfect location for a walking tour. To get around the city the easiest way is to walk, since its dimension allows it. Walk on the Passeig Maritimpromenade and enjoy the view on the historical city and the light breeze from the sea. For further points like the Playa del Muerto, make your way with a taxi. Sitges disposes of a train station with straight TRAINS TO AND FROM BARCELONA, which makes it accessible for a DAY TRIP during your STAY IN THE CATALAN CAPITAL.

Quick Guide to Sitges

Understanding

Sitges is a lovely Mediterranean coastal town, a seaside resort some 35km southwest of Barcelona in Catalunya, Spain. Sitges is a seaside town with great beaches and excellent tourist facilities. Recognized as one of the most charming towns and prestige of the Catalan coast, enjoys a mild and temperate micro climate, which means that visitors can enjoy enviable temperatures every month of the year Sitges has one of most vibrant and hippest gay scenes on the coast. The beaches are very colorful and fun! The city which overlooks the Mediterranean has large avenues, narrow streets, four museums and the gorgeous beaches of Costa Dorada/Golden Coast

Sitges is a unique enclave on the Mediterranean coast, protected by the Garraf's Parc mountains. With 300 days of sunshine per year, Sitges has an excellent microclimate that allows you to enjoy this beautiful coastal town. Throughout the year there are countless events, such as: the Sitges International Film Festival, Sitges Carnival, local festivities, Theatre Festival, Vintage car rally, Gay Pride, concerts and more. Sitges is home to many cultural and artistic activities and numerous art galleries and craft stores. Together with a vibrant nightlife, any visit promises to be unforgettable.

A few minutes from the city of Barcelona (35km) and Barcelona, El Prat International Airport (25 km), Sitges is an unbeatable option for both private or corporate holidays. The region can also be accessed from Reus and Girona airports with low cost airlines flying from many European airports.

Sitges is a large village (about 44 sq km) in Garraf, in the Barcelona province in the autonomous region of Catalonia. It has more than 28,000 inhabitants, of whom about 30% are non-native, which gives the town a very special character and charm.

Sitges is a maritime town. It has a large tourist infrastructure and facilities. With three local marinas, it has more than any other town in Spain. In addition to tourism, there are fishing and shoe-making and artistic businesses, though the former now consist of smaller workshops. The town was rebuilt in the last century, to accommodate increased tourism. There are some 13 individually named beaches along a 2.5km promenade.

Noted for its outstanding location, the Church of Sant Bartomeu i Santa Tecla, better known as "La

Punta" at the end of the promenade in a bastion above steps and a coastal cliff, has become one of the most recognized icons in Sitges, much photographed and painted. Its structure is quite peculiar, because it has two bell towers, and possesses one of the watch towers that served the population to calculate the time. Its facade is quite simple but the frame where it is located is incomparable. The beautiful parish of San Bartolome and Santa Tecla is certainly the image that symbolizes Sitges. The church, built in the seventeenth century but with many subsequent amendments, is a charming Baroque style and the interior retains several Renaissance and Baroque altars and an organ of 1690.

El Raco de la Calma is a really lovely place to pass by sen route from the beach of San Sebastian to the church of Sant Bertomeu and Santa Tecla. Walking through the Racó you will find the most beautiful and relaxing places in Sitges, as musicians help the relaxation and tranquility to appreciate. At the end of this walk in a large square overlooking the sea and the lighthouse there is a very nice market where we can buy accessories, earrings, clothes, bracelets .

Sitges is a wonderful place to spend a great summer on its magnificent beaches and to roam around its magnificent streets.

From Barcelona:

The easiest way is by the Spanish Railways (RENFE , "Rodalies de Catalunya"). The journey by train (R2 Sud) from Barcelona costs €4,20 (single) or €8,40 8return) (4 Zones on the Barcelona suburban railway services), and takes around 35 minutes. Direct trains leave from Passeig de Gràcia; Sants and Estació de França stations - from Plaça de Catalunya (L1 Metro) change at Barcelona-Sants. There are four trains an hour - two fast trains and two stopping trains. From Plaça de Catalunya there is a night bus service (Mon-Bus) when normal bus service stops at about 10:30 PM.

By car, there are two routes - either via the C-31 (a local road which winds its way around the cliff faces) or the C-32 (a toll motorway). The C-32 is recommended for speed and safety, however it costs around €6, while the C-31 is free.

By Air, the closest international airport is Barcelona/El Prat de Llobregat(BCN) airport (Sitges is accessible by train from Terminal 2 via Rodalies mainline or Metro L9 services or T1 via Metro L9. Both require changing at El Prat de Llobregat stations. Reus/Tarragona(REU) airport is an alternative,for regional flights (Sitges is accessible by train changing at either Sant Vicenç de Calders or Vilanova i la Geltrú).Girona/Gerona(GRO) airport is over 125 km in Costa Brava.

To Get around

Walk or taxi cab; it is a charming small city.Sitges allows the movement of vehicles for their urban fabric, only some of the streets near "Cap de la Vila", the inner city, have limited to motor vehicle traffic, allowing pedestrians and cycling. There are several bus lines that serve communication with the various developments that surround the town of Sitges. It may be interesting to park the car at any of the park and ride there and I walk closer to the center, and especially advisable in the months of July and August to avoid driving on the center with the car. The best way is rent a electric Bike.

To See

For its rich cultural diversity allows different tourist routes that show as the passage of time has left its mark on this beach town so special. Known tourist routes in Sitges and are therefore recommended as the tourism promotion agency as those made by AGIS, are the "Indianos Route", Sitges in Time of Modernism Route, Sitges Old Town, The Souls Route, Terramar Route, Route de la Malvasia, La Ruta de las Mujeres de Sitges and its proximity to the Parc del Garraf is also recommended Route dels Sentits Garraf.

Interestingly distracted by corners that Sitges has to offer and is highly recommended especially starting Ride La Fragata, climb to the church Sant Bartomeu i Santa Tecla and continue walking in the Raco de la Calma, past museums Maricel,

Cau Ferrat and reach the tranquil beach of San Sebastian.

Sitges Holidays and Traditions Sitges offers visitors not only a pleasant and pretty coastal village and magnificent spaces for visiting Sitges also offers many events, activities, festivals that make its cultural and artistic life transcend beyond the Mediterranean's Sea waters.

They are internationally known its International Film Festival, The Carnival, The Gay Pride, Classic Car Rally Barcelona-Sitges, The International Tango Festival, and popular folk character, but no less attractive highlights La Festa Major de Sant Bartomeu, the Festa Major de Santa Tecla, El Corpus, La Nit de Foc, Mare de Deu del Carme, The Verema....

Cau Ferrat: this house was owned by Santiago Russiñol, a modernist painter that gave a lot of life to the movement. many parties where held here, and now you can see paintings, sculptures, etc. the name comes from Cau, ("place") and ferrat, ("made of iron"), since the place has many decorative items made of these materials.

This museum has a small Picasso, several el Grecos as well as some small pieces by a range of Catalan modernists.

To Do

Sitges has 17 beaches adorning the coastline of Sitges, some close to the village center and other far, more dispersed , but all of them have the necessary services. There are great beaches, small coves, family beaches, naturist beaches.... Urban beaches are easily reached on foot from the beautiful promenade. Six of these beaches were honored recently with the ISO 14001 certification for the quality of water, sand, cleaning services, lifesaving.

Sitges Food and Drink Sitges offers visitors an extraordinary cuisine, where Mediterranean cuisine such high regard that world has acquired in recent times is exalted. Rice, fresh fish, famous xató, ... The tasting Mediterranean cuisine is very pleasant in the seafront in Sitges. It should be noted the Malvasia de Sitges, as sweet dessert wine, aromatic, made from the grape variety of the same name. Malvasia de Sitges today enjoys international recognition thanks to the action of Slow Food. We should not go to Sitges without having tasted the typical Spanish tapas in one of the many tapas establishments that offer discounts for all visitors to Sitges.

Santa Tecla Festival. between 15th and 23rd September. One of the most important Spanish traditional festival, between 15th and 23rd September. It has been celebrated since 1321 and it has been considered of national touristic interest by Spanish government. Human towers, historical parades and fireworks are some of the main activities.

➢ Sitges Film Festival

To Buy

Buy Sitges Sitges has a wide range of shops, the town center streets are full of small shops that allow consumers to meet their consumption needs. The Main Street, The Parellades street, The Cap de la Vila, Jesus Street, the Sant Francesc street, ... are some of the most commercial streets of the town center. There are various craftworks products Sitges, are famous miniature reproductions of the most characteristic elements of the Local Festa Major.

In Sitges (unlike nearby Barcelona) all of the shops are allowed to open on Sundays. You will find a wide range of fashion stores around the city. Several of them carry top brands. Pedestrian streets on the city center get quite crowded on Sunday afteroons with tourists and people from Barcelona buying. Be aware that several shops on the afternoon open just after 17:30 and stay open untill 21:00.

La Garriga: (Tel. +0034 938531122. Espalter Street, 9, 08870 Sitges) Delicatessen shopping store set up in 1965 and renovated in 2016. La Garriga keeps its essence and tradition of selling the best cured ham in downtown. Since the last shopping store renovation, you also can find fantastic high-quality fresh food and gastronomic souvenirs to bring them back home such us delicatessen, cheeses, meat, fruit and vegetables and a wide range of wines.

To Eat

Sitges offers a wide range of restaurants. You will find that best suits your taste. The Mediterranean cuisine is offered in most establishments in high quality level. Highly recommended to try tapas establishments.

Fragata Paseig de la Ribera (under the old church). One of the best fine dining restaurants in Sitges with wonderful harbour views and stunning food. Inspired by the local fish and seafood but delivered with a style and flair that sets it apart.

To Drink

Sitges Pubs streets near the waterfront are filled with street cafes. Local youngsters gather on the beach after nightfall.

Sitges has great range of bars and places in which to enjoy a drink, a wine, a beer in the company of his acquaintances friends. Night pubs in the Port of Aiguadolç, the Sweet Pacha , Disco Atlantida, but undoubtedly the place par excellence of nightlife is "Sin street - La Calle del Pecado" and popularly known by the concentration of bars and nightlife venues. You can not go off Sitges without having enjoyed its nightlife.

Rainbow Bar, Carrer de Sant Pau 34, Sitges, 08870, Spain, 34.655.712.272, . 12 Noon. Rainbow Bar is the bar & restaurant of Casa Rainbow Sitges. It offers your favorite cocktail and a different tapas menu daily, live music, shows and the Sunday's Tea Time bingo. It is open from 12 noon nonstop until 2 in the morning, seven days a week. A complimentary drink is offered to Casa Rainbow guests. euros 5.

To Sleep

Sitges has over 5,000 beds to accommodate the many tourists who hosts. The hotel offer covers all tastes and prices, from large hotels from large chains to those small boutique hotels and family service. Tourists also enjoy a generous offer apartments for rent.

Andy's Rooms >> , San Juan, Sitges - Located in the heart of the old town, gay owned and operated. Beautiful rooms in a 500 year old Catalan Casa,

Hotel Celimar >> , Passeig De La Ribera, 18. Tel. (+34) 93 811 01 70. Modest rooms, with bath & shower, facing onto the beach front, about 30 minutes drive or train west out of Barcelona. About €100 per night for a double room.

Merráneo Sitges · Hotel & Apartments >> This 4 stars apartment-hotel is in a great location right on the beachfront. The apartments have a bedroom, lounge, marble bathroom, kitchen and private terrace. You are directly on the beach and a short walk from the town centre.

Hotel Sunway Playa Golf Sitges >>, Paseo Marítimo 92-94, +34 93 894 18 39 (, fax: +34 93 894 14 64), . checkin: noon; checkout: noon. On the Sitges Promenade, by the sea and next to the golf course. 4-star hotel with doubles, studios or fully equipped apartments, most of them with sea views.

Sitges Hills Villas >> (http://www.sitgeshillsvillas.com/), Avinguda del Port d'Aiguadolç, 4 08870 Sitges, +34 659 516 745 (email -), . A collection of luxury designer holiday villas and beautiful farmhouses with private swimming pools in and around the town of Sitges.

InSitges Apartments >> (InSitges), Carrer Port Alegre, 39 (Platja Sant Sebastià), +34 607 248 011, . Apartments by the sea, on San Sebastia beach, downtown Sitges. Fully equipped with kitchens, air conditioning and everything you need for a perfect holiday. Two bedrooms per apartment, with an option for a sofa bed in the lounge.

Sitges Apartments >> (Sitges Holiday Accommodation), Paseo de la Ribera, 44, +34 670 307 510, . A local run and owned business with over 50 properties in Sitges ranging from basic studios to luxury villas. from 60eur/night.

Casa Rainbow Sitges >>, Carrer de Sant Pau 34, Sitges 08870, Spain, 34.655.712.272, . checkin: 2PM; checkout: 12 Noon. Casa Rainbow Sitges provides all the perks as any other 5 stars hotel in a home atmosphere. Casa Rainbow Sitges a

Boutique Guest house offers suites and Penthouses that includes toiletries, daily cleaning service, Free Wi-Fi, flat panel Television, on-suite music and daily continental breakfast included in the rate. Casa Rainbow Sitges is located in the center of the town just a few steps from the beach. Euros 150.

Hotel Masia Sumidors >>, Carretera de Vilafranca, km 4.6, Sant Pere de Ribes, 08810 Barcelona, Spain (phone="+34938962061"), . checkin: 14.00; checkout: 12.00. Only ten minutes outside Sitges, nestled in the Garraf National Park, is Hotel Masia Sumidors. One of only two hotels within the Park, this 400 year old Catalan Masia is a perfect rustic, rural retreat. With a swimming pool and bar and breathtaking views over the vineyards and valleys, this is perfect for a romantic getaway or relaxing break. Hotel Masia Sumidors is relaxed, informal, friendly and welcoming. Complimentary Cava on arrival, Free Wifi & Free Parking. from €80.

Casita Sitges >>, carrer de l'aigua 21, sobreático, +34648013914, . Casita Sitges is a charming holiday boutique apartment in the heart of Sitges old town next to San Sebastian beach. The apartment is decorated in a fresh, elegant and creative mediterranean style with a sea view terrace with an outdoor hot shower and a second terrace with a brick barbecue. The Casita can host up to 4 guests has one bedroom, a sofa bed in the living room, two bathroom and an equipped kitchen. There are two bikes available for its guests, free unlimited Wifi internet, and bed linen, towels and beach towels included in the rate. From 85€/night.

Museums

Cau Ferrat Museum

The Museum of Cau Ferrat is located in SITGES, the famous Catalan beach resort. Cau Ferrat lies on the coast of SANT SEBASTIAN, one of Sitges' most popular BEACHES. The museum was founded as a home workshop of Santiago Rusiñol, the leader of the Catalan modernism movement. It contains collections of ancient and modern art gathered from well-known artists such as Pablo Picasso and Rusiñol himself.

Rusiñol was part of a middle-class family and was meant to follow the family's tradition to become a cotton manufacturer. Rusiñol chose to follow a different path, and decided to join the (Artistic Scene Of Catalonia). Sitges was the place chosen by Rusiñol to spread his religious theory of the total art when art is considered to be a religion. The movement made Sitges the Vatican of

Modernism and Rusiñol the Pope of the movement. He aimed to transform society through art and culture, and he was able to create whole mythology around his figure.

The building was left on a will to God, and after authorization of sale from the Ecclesiastical Court of the Diocese of Barcelona in 1893, the house was sold. Rusiñol renewed the place to make it his home and studio, and named it Cau Ferrat, as it was the name of the studio he had lived at in Barcelona. One year later, he bought the house next doors and incorporated it into the building as we know it nowadays. In 1895 he celebrated the 3rd Festa Modernista, the cultural event largely celebrating modernistic wave. He scheduled it on the same day he received two paintings by El Greco he had acquired in France a few months earlier.

Nowadays the museum has collections of paintings, drawings, and iron sculptures, which are made up by Rusiñol's favorite pieces, the ones he had an emotional connection with. Many pieces of famous Catalan artists are also exposed, such as Pablo Picasso and Ramon Casas. The artwork represents Rusiñol's personal tastes and preferences and also many of the time's trends in art. Most of the work was done by the artist himself. The museum has a collection of glassware that has over 400 pieces acquired by him. It is divided into a modern and antique glass collection. The furniture and sculptures are also part of the collection, although they might pass unnoticed as decorative pieces. The museum also exhibits a wide collection of ceramics with over 200 pieces concentrated mainly on the ground floor of the house.

Museu Cau Ferrat is one of SITGES' main museums and is located downtown the village. There are various options for getting to Sitges from the city of Barcelona. The fastest option is a 30 minutes train ride, but it is also convenient to take a bus running late at night as well.

How to get there?

BY TRAIN: The C2 train travels to Sitges from stations Estació de França, Passeig de Gràcia, and Estació Sants. However, not every train goes from Estació de França, therefore it is best to check the timetable if you wish to travel from that station. The train operates between 6:47 and 19:37. A single journey costs €4.10 and return journey €7.20.

BY BUS: Buses to Sitges from Barcelona leave from Plaça España and Ronda Universitat during the day. They are run by a bus company called

MonBus. The night buses operation between 0:55 and 5:51 run from Plaça de Catalunya under numbers N30, N31 or N32. A single journey costs €4.10.

BY CAR: There are two options for getting to Sitges from Barcelona by car. The first one is a scenic route along the coast, meanwhile, the second one is a motorway C-32. The second option is faster, however, you have to pay a toll.

Museum Maricel

The artistic complex of Maricel was built between 1910 and 1918 by Miquel Utrillo. The building was built for the American Charles Deering who wanted a home to serve all his needs and shelter his artwork. The place used to be a hospital and was converted into a residence. Deering still wasn't satisfied, so he acquired all the fishermen houses. He wanted his art collection to have the respectful environment they deserved. Due to the renovations, the entire neighborhood's image was changed. Utrillo got inspiration from Cau Ferrat and Can Llopis, two other buildings that are museums in Sitges.

The art collection that was first exposed in the house had mostly Hispanic artists as a focus, and some other pieces that Deering acquired in other places. The most important ones from the gothic selection included El Greco, Vicente Lopez, Viladomat and Goya. The modernist pieces were represented by Ramon Casas, Regoyos, Santiago Rusiñol and the modern sculptures by Enric Casanovas and Gustave Violet and many more. After many seasons and becoming Sitges' "Adoptive Son", Charles Deering left Sitges in 1921 after disagreements with Utrillo.

With that, the art collection was donated partially to the Art Institute of Chicago, and the other part was left under the Deering family's ownership. Some other pieces were transferred to the castle of Tamarit, which Deering had acquired in 1916. After that, the building was used for many things that weren't its initial purpose, until the museums board of Sitges rented it to expand the exhibition from Cau Ferrat Museum. In 1954 the complex was sold to the town hall and in 1969 Charles Deering's former residence to place the art collection donated by Dr. Jesus Perez-Rosales.

Today, the museum shows artwork from the 10th to the 20th century through Dr. Perez-Rosale's collection and the city's. The pieces that were owned by Dr. Jesus were never exposed before, and were incorporated with donations from artists' families. The complex includes the

Museum Maricel; Can Rocamora that connects the Maricel and the Cau Ferrat; Palau Maricel, in front of the two other buildings; Biblioteca Popular Santiago Rusiñol, inaugurated in 1936; and the Arxiu Històric de Sitges, on the ground floor.

The Museum Maricel today is situated where Charles Deering used to live. It is made up of more than 3000 pieces from different origins that include Romanesque murals, Gothic paintings, Renaissance carvings, Modernist and Novocentist sculptures, canvas and several pictures and pieces of furniture. The museum organise various activites, exhibitions and collections,

Address: Calle Fonollar, 08870 Sitges
Opening hours: *1. March 30. June and 1. 31. October:* Tuesday Sunday from 10:00am to

7:00pm

1. July 30. September: Tuesday Sunday from 10:00am to 8:00pm

1. November 28. February: Tuesday Sunday from 10:00am to 5:00pm

Tickets: 5€, various discounts applies

How to get there:

Car: 42 km, approximately 45 minutes, check the CAR COMPANIES and hire one!

Train: Linie R2 South from Barcelona Sants or Estació de Franca, 45 minutes

Bus: MonBus Line from Ronda Universitat

Carnival of Sitges

The religious holiday Carnival is celebrated all around the world. Carnival is when you have the last chance to be naughty before lent. The Carnival of SITGES is one of the most popular ones in Catalonia. Its history is over 100 years old. On the 15th century, a dyslexic man misspelled Carles de Can Torras for Calrestorles. Calrestorles died on an Ash Wednesday, the first day of Lent. With time and people's imagination, the people of Sitges made Calrestorles be remembered as Carnestoltes. For that reason, Fat Thursday has the King Carnestoltes arriving with the Queen to the city to proclaim unlimited partying, and the last day, Ash Wednesday, the burial of Carnestoltes is celebrated, where the testament is read.

Those events are all performances that go around the city in parades with symbolic meanings. The parades have people dressed up in costumes that represent different roles in the performance. During the weekend of Carnival, there are several visits from the Queen and children queen of carnival to schools, nursing and senior homes in the city. On Sunday, there is a parade dedicated to children and a parade dedicated to adults with typical dances. People that take part on the parade take their costumes seriously. Feathers, glitter, makeup, are all fundamental on a good costume for the Sitges Parade.

Every year the Carnival of Sitges attracts around 250,000 people from all around the world in addition to the city's population. People of all ages and genders come to the "pueblo" to enjoy the week's festivities. Most of these temporary tourists come for A DAY from their STAY IN BARCELONA by TRAIN or bus, since Sitges is only 30km away from the Catalan capital.

Due to Sitges' popularity for being a famous gay destination and the openness of the locals to the gay community, the carnival of Sitges is more adult focused than family focused, however many families and kids still participate on the day parades and kids-only parades. The largest parades take place on Sunday and Shrove Tuesday. The most popular parades are the Debauchery Parade and the Extermination Parade. Debauchery is famous for its 40 floats that carry over 2,000 participants during its course. The Extermination Parade marks the end of celebrations. It is usually full with drag queens dressed in black in grief for the death of the king of carnival. Finally, on Ash Wednesday, the Burial of the Sardine, or the king, symbolizes the beginning of the abstinence period.

Guys in Sitges

Gay Bars in Sitges

The beautiful Spanish coastal town of Sitges has been a POPULAR GAY DESTINATION for decades.

In addition to the wide offer of GAY BEACHES and vibrant gay bars in Sitges, the town has also another big advantage. It's just 30 minutes by train from Barcelona, a city with an endless number of sights to explore and A THRIVING BAR SCENE to experience.

The Sitges gay bar scene is busy all year round. The main season is from May to end of September. Most of the bars open from the beginning of Spring (March 20th). As Easter arrives the bars open daily as do the discos and clubs. Off season Sitges is still well worth a visit with bars in the city centre open from Thursdays to Sundays.

Are you planning to spend an unforgettable night in Sitges and get a first hand experience of local gay culture? Our roundup of the most popular gay bars in Sitges can surely help.

Parrots Pub

Parrots bar is located in the centre of Sitges and the terrace is the perfect place to watch the world go by. The bar attracts all age groups. Trendy youngsters mixing it up with locals and their admirers to bears during "Bears week". The bar is busy everyday and the staff are very friendly.

During the season (March to October) Parrots is open 7 days a week, the Pub from 8.30am, serving a delicious breakfast and the terrace opens from 5pm. Don't forget to get there early to find the perfect seat finding a free spot is really difficult in Parrots. After their sunbaths, many tourists walk from the beach passing by the Carrer del Pecat (literally Sin's Street) where Parrots has its terrace.

Address: Plaça de la Indústria, 2, 08870 Sitges

Comodin Bar

One of the most popular gay bars in Sitges, the Comodín Bar is well known thanks to its Drag Queens shows. The bar gets busy from early on, so make sure you get there early to get the best vantage point for the shows.

Comodin Bar is one of the first bars of gay friendly Sitges, its beginnings go back to the early 60's. A place that is always partying, where you can enjoy their live shows every night from the months of June to September. The rest of the year offers the shows on Friday and Saturday nights. Many parties throughout the year are celebrated at Comodin, but one that you should not miss, is the Festival of La Mantilla, where you'll experience the true spirit of this place.

Address: Carrer d'en Tacó 4, 08870 Sitges

Casablanca

A bar where conversation, background music, jazz and emblematic songs from many different eras, mix with traditional and stylish cocktails as well as nice wines. This venue opts for a different music style, while others play pop or house hits, Casablanca prefers jazz, not very loud, so you can enjoy the relaxing atmosphere. Thanks to that, Casablanca's the perfect spot to chill while having a chat with friends, or a romantic date, while drinking a glass of wine (be aware of their great wine selection!).

The Casablanca cocktail bar is run by local couple Juan and Brandon who have owned the place since 1998. A cozy locale with an intimate lounge area decorated with local art on the first floor, the bar hosts regular French-themed nights with plenty of pate and cheese. Casablanca offers an altogether much more relaxed atmosphere than the other Sitges gay bars.

Address: Carrer d'en Pau Barrabeig, 5, 08870 Sitges

The Gay Beaches of Sitges

On the Golden coast of SITGES you will find 22 beautiful beaches. Of those 22 beaches, 3 of them are gay beaches. The gay beaches of Sitges are called Playa de la Bassa Rodona, Playa de las Balmins and Playa del Muerto. Continue reading to find out which beach is best suited for you!

Which Beach is the Best for You?

Playa de la Bassa Rodona

Playa de la Bassa Rodona is Stiges' main and most well known gay beach. Bassa Rodona is a fairly thin sand strip, with a length of 285 meters and an average width of just under 20 meters. The beach has everything you could need; there are lifeguards on duty as well as facilities such as toilets, the renting of parasols, deck chairs, kayaks, even massage services. The beach is cleaned regularly and the calm waters make it a blue flag beach. Right across from the famous Hotel "Calipolis", this beach can be easily spotted from the amount of speedos and tanned masculine bodies. For refreshments, a beach bar and the popular Restaurant Picnic offer a wide variety of drinks and cocktails.

Platja dels Balmins

The other two gay beaches in Sitges are naturist. Platja dels Balmins is situated on the east side of the town, right before the port, Port D'Aiguadolç. Although it used to be exclusively straight, the wide acceptance of the gay community by the locals soon led to it becoming a beach inclusive to everyone. The nudity at Balmins is not mandatory, so you can still enjoy the beach with swimwear or clothes on. There is a great view of the beach from the little restaurant above it, for those who want a meal after a long day at the beach while watching the sun set over the sea.

Playa del Muerto

The other gay beach in Sitges is Playa del Muerto. This beach is also naturist but more private, located at the bottom of a small cliff and further away from the city center. The difficulty of accessing it makes it live up to its name "Dead Man's Beach". Don't worry if you're coming from far away, as it is possible to access the area by car. After you park your car, there are two walking paths up to the shore, one short and one long. The short path is steep and goes down the side of the cliff, perfect for anyone who is a bit adventurous! The longer path is beside some train tracks. The trip down to Playa del Muerto takes a bit longer than getting to the other beaches, so if you want to spend time at all of these beaches you might want to consider a longer stay in Sitges to get the most out of your visit.

Both nudist beaches have areas known for *cruising*. At Playa de las Balmins, the cruising spot is in the tunnel behind the beach where the train tracks pass through. At Playa del Muerto, the designated area is in the woods behind the train tracks, where it becomes full of people as the sun sets. In the gay community, cruising is the term used for the search of a casual sex partner.

The Gay Community of Sitges

According to the Merriam-Webster dictionary, one of the definitions for the word "Gay" is: happy and excited; cheerful and lively. That's how you can describe SITGES. Located 35km south of Barcelona, Sitges is probably the most popular gay destination in Spain. The gay community of Sitges meets the straight community and every sexual orientation blends in. Gay men and women from all over the world come to Sitges to enjoy their holidays without the pretentious looks of discrimination they get in other places.

The gay attractiveness of Sitges starts back in the '80s when the first gay club of Spain was opened. Now a day, the number of gay-friendly establishments has grown to several, and among hotels, bars and clubs, the gay community is warmly welcomed in Sitges. The most popular beach is the Playa de la Bassa Rodona. Although that is considered *the* gay beach, all beaches are tolerant and gay-friendly. There are two nudist beaches in Sitges: Playa de las Balmins and Playa del Muerto, the latter being exclusively gay. Along the seaside road, Passeig Maritim, many events are hosted. The most popular one being the Gay Pride Parade, which takes place every year. The parade is free for everyone to attend, and the after parties in the gay village is also free of charge.

Another event that takes place on the streets of Sitges is the CARNIVAL. During its week, it attracts over 250,000 people that dress up in costumes and wander its streets partying. Besides Carnival, other religious holidays are also celebrated with a gay twist, such as Easter (40 days after Carnival) and Corpus Christi. Towards the end of summer, in September, another popular event that takes place is the Bears Week. In the gay culture, a Bear is a large, hairy man that shows an image of masculinity. The event attracts over 5,000 people over a period of two weeks.

There are no gay exclusive hotels in Sitges, so it would be interesting to RENT AN APARTMENT with friends. The most popular location is nearby the gay beach, Playa de la Bassa Rodona. Other popular hangout locations also include the city's two saunas: Parrots Sauna, located at the Parrots Sitges Hotel and Sauna Sitges at the Pension Espalter, and the Carrer del Pecat ("street of sin"), which is actually called Carrer 1er de Maig. That is where the Pacha's official pub is located, the Pachito.

During the high or low season, the fun is guaranteed all year round in Sitges. The perfect state of harmony and comfort from the local community is what attracts the gay population. Sitges is the perfect spot to enjoy the amazing weather Spain has to offer, along with the hottest events in the region.

Traditional Gastronomy in Sitges

There are a wide variety of typical products in Sitges ranging from decoration items and clothing to culinary dishes. We would like to highlight the following:

One of the better-known gastronomical products of the area is the Malvasía de Sitges. It is produced in various formats: the most renowned is a sweet, fragrant passito (dessert wine) with a 15% alcoholic content. A dry fortified wine is also made, along with a sparkling wine and an aromatic white wine, all of them produced exclusively from the Malvasia grape from which the wines take their name. In the eighteenth century the Malvasia grape made up ¼ of the crops cultivated in Sitges, although now there are only 2,5 hectares under cultivation. The Slow Food Foundation for Biodiversity has included the Malvasia de Sitges in its Ark of Taste list (small-scale quality productions under threat).

Sitges Malvasia is a true rarity: even if it is included in the 84 internationally recognized varieties of Malvasia, only a few hectares of this production survive. The good news is that this increasingly valued grape variety is being extended into other vineyards in the Penedès area. The chalky soil, marine breeze and protection offered by the mountains all contribute to a unique microclimate favourable to the Sitges Malvasía. The small, elongated grapes are allowed to overripen and are picked at the end of September-beginning of October.

Sitges diplomat Manuel Llopis i de Casades (1885-1935) bequeathed his land including a couple of hectares of Malvasía vines in Aiguadolç, his wine business and most of the

Llopis family properties to the Sant Joan Baptista Hospital of Sitges provided the commitment was made (and which is still honoured today) to continue quality production of the Malvasia wine. Today production stands at around 4,000 litres per year.

Malvasía de Sitges, Hospital de Sant Joan de Sitges, D.O. Penedès, can be purchased in various establishments around town such as specialised wine shops, cake shops and gourmet stores.

Sitges style rice (Arròs a la Sitgetana)

Because of its bonds with the sea, the varied gastronomy of Sitges is closely related to seafood and rice dishes. It's remarkable the called "Arros a la Sitgetana" a dish retrieved by Emerencià Roig i Raventos in his book published in 1934 "El Sitges dels nostres avis" (The Sitges of our grandparents), a compilation of oral traditions about the 19th century life in Sitges including some references to the dishes that were formerly cooked in Sitges.

This is a dish based on rice to which some seafood and products from the countryside are added. Check the recipe at right.

El Xató:

Xató is a local dish that features a dressing made from toasted almonds, toasted hazel nuts, bread, ripe tomatoes, vinegar, garlic, oil, salt and ñora. (The ñora is a type of sun-dried sweet pepper, burgundy/purple in colour, about the size of a garlic glove, popular along the Spanish Mediterranean coast. When rehydrated the resulting thin flesh is scraped away from the skin and used in cooking.) The dressing, of a thick consistency, decorates a salad of escarola (curly endive), anchovies, tuna, rehydrated and desalinated cod and olives. Various towns and villages in the Penedès and Garraf area lay claim to the ownership of this seasonal salad and hold xatonadas (yearly xató festivals open to all) to enjoy and promote the local speciality. Many restaurants have xató on their menu. There are also various establishments in Sitges where you may purchase the ready-made sauce such as the municipal market and shops with food to go...

Where to buy:
Establishments where to purchase the ingredients for traditional recipes or to buy ready-made food:

The charcutería Fontanals which offers a wide selection of local cold cuts including the botifarra d'ou, meat, cheese...

Across the road is Xamaní, a well stocked fruit and vegetable shop which also offers dairy products and some ready-made dishes. Xamaní also sells the xató dressing in conveniently sealed bags.

Next to Xamani is Vi més Vi, a specialized wine shop where you can savour a glass of wine and have a little nibble. The shop stocks local wines as well as some international wines.

In the Sitges Municipal Market (next to the train station), on Calle Artur Carbonell: There are a wide variety of establishments in the market offering quality produce: fruit, vegetables, cold cuts, meat, fish, regional products etc. One of the market stalls that sells cod will also prepare the xató sauce.

All supermarkets stock the packaged xató sauce, normally presented in a jar. The most commonly available brand is by Ferrer, however it is not homemade.

The Best Tapas Restaurants in Sitges

There is a great tradition of tapas in Sitges. Not only that the town hosts the winning restaurant of "Catalonia's tapa of the year", but it also hosts the "Tapa a Tapa" and "The Tapa of the year" events which are some of the greatest gastronomic happenings in Catalonia. Tapas is the name of different small Spanish appetizers that you can enjoy before a big meal, or simply serve for dinner.

Tapas can be small plates of food or big plates of food. Mediterranean countries like Spain have a tradition to serve a selection of many small dishes at once. And since the Spaniards and the Latin Americans are truly sociable, tapas are an inherent part of the national culture.

Tapas dishes are often eaten as a light snack with beer, wine or sherry or as a starter enjoyed comfortably while the food is being prepared. In Spain and Sitges, many people might prefer to enjoy it with a glass of sangria or cava. Tapas consists of several sorts of food, such as garlic tomato, baguette, olives, ham, sausages, and bruschetta just to mention a few.

As it's mainly a social affair, tapas are served during family meetings and meetings with friends. This dish often includes a glass of good wine, that's why you can enjoy tapas when in wine bars or restaurants. But bars and nightclubs are not an exception so as you can see, the Spanish really love tapas so you can get them everywhere!

In Sitges you will find many restaurants serving this delicious local food. The serving of tapas is designed to encourage conversation because people are not so focused upon eating an entire meal that is set before them. Take a look at the list of the best tapas restaurants in Sitges that are worth trying!

El Pou

A tapas restaurant El Pou is situated in the very center of Sitges. Their philosophy is to serve Spanish cuisine to people with a clear commitment to quality and service, all this for affordable prices. The menu includes a wide variety of traditional tapas, original tapas or typical Catalan «Coca» bread. What is especially worth trying is the tuna tataki and the wajyu burger. So when in Sitges, this authentic tapas restaurant is certainly a must-visit!

Address: Carrer de Sant Bonaventura, 21, 08870 Sitges

El Cable

This tapas bar in Sitges was opened in 1940 and is currently run by the third generation of the Andreu family. What is truly remarkable is the bar's success in various competitions for the best tapas in town El Cable won this title four times! Moreover, in 2013, the bar won the prize for the best tapas in Cataloniawith "Buscant en Nemo", a tuna tartar. This place is not just a bar, it's a local meeting point for many people in Sitges who wish to enjoy a great meal in a cozy atmosphere. If you visit El Cable, you just can't miss their Patatas Bravas and the award-winning "Buscant en Nemo".

Address: Carrer Barcelona, 1, 08870 Sitges

El Trull

An iconic restaurant in Sitges that preserves good cuisine with a professional chef who constantly studies dishes with an excellent quality. At El

Trull you'll get a truly local and rustic feeling. You're just a step away from ordering specialties of the Spanish traditional cuisine such as goat cheese salad or exquisite chocolate mousse, which is really the perfect icing on the cake to complete their delicious menu. The intimate and relaxed atmosphere inside with the combination of a beautiful and romantic terrace outside that's the perfect way to end your day!

Address: Passatge Mossèn Fèlix Clarà, 3, 08870 Sitges

The Information You Need For a Successful Day Trip To Sitges

SITGES is located about 30 km south of Barcelona and is one of the most popular resorts in Southern Europe. It's packed in summer, mostly by young Northern Europeans. The resort has largely drawn prosperous middle-class industrialists from Barcelona for years, but those old days are gone. Sitges has long been known as a city of cultural value, thanks to its residential artists, such as the Bohemian mystic SANTIAGO RUSINOL. The town is bursting at the seams with famous art deco buildings, and the seafront promenade is lined with palm trees. Its 17 beaches are some of the best on the Mediterranean coastline.

Sitges is mostly a BEACH destination; however, it does have a handful of other attractions to offer. These include three museums dedicated to art and old artifacts, a cinema, an old cemetery, and a beautifully renovated CHURCH. Sitges' microclimate gives you an average of 300 sunshine days a year. It also hosts significant film, dance and culture festivals such as Fantástico and THE CARNIVAL. Sitges is worth visiting all year round.

History

The 19th Century modernism movement began primarily in Sitges, and the town remained the playground of artistic encounters and demonstrations long after the movement waned. Sitges continued to be a resort for artists, attracting the likes of Salvador Dalí and poet Federico García Lorca. The Spanish Civil War erased what has come to be called the "golden age" of Sitges. Although other artists and writers arrived in the decades to follow, none had the name or impact of those who had gone before.

Festivals in Sitges

As with all Spanish towns, festivals make up an essential part of Sitges' culture. The town hosts a varied array of FESTIVALS. Throughout the year festivals include a tango festival, a cinema festival, and a vintage car festival. Without a doubt, Sitges' most legendary festival is Mardi

Gras in February. The streets become filled with carnival processions and people wearing fancy dresses for a whole week. It is one of the best times to be in town.

Sitges' Carnival is one of the figureheads of the Catalán calendar. For more than a century, the town celebrates the days before the beginning of Lent. People are dressed up in fancy all over Sitges and Barcelona, floats, feathered outfits, and sequins spice up this event. The party begins on the Thursday before Lent with the arrival of the King of the Carnestoltes and ends with the Entierro de la Sardina -Burial of Sardine- on Ash Wednesday. This is a symbolical burial of the past to allow society to be reborn, transformed and with new vigor. Activities reach their flamboyant climax on Sant Bonaventura where the GAY COMMUNITY holds their celebrations.

Activities

There are many activities to do on your day trip to Sitges. For bike riding, there are numerous bicycle hire shops all over Sitges. Why not play some golf on a cold afternoon. The three closest golf clubs to Sitges are Vinyet mini-golf, Terramar golf course, and CTC golf club. There are also tennis clubs which enable you to play tennis throughout the local sports centers in Sitges. Additional activities include jet-skiing, sailing, charter schools, and other water sports. Finally, there are several beaches in Sitges, 17 to be precise and three pools where you can laze about on a sunny afternoon.

Beaches

The beaches in the city are lively and clean. They are sandy with clean Mediterranean water and well served, with walkways to the waterfront and chiringuitos (beach huts; small bar-restaurants) selling food, drinks and pedalo hire. Behind the beaches is a picturesque promenade, followed by rows of restaurants, bars, and ice-cream parlors. In general, all the beaches are both family and gay-friendly. However, certain beaches are considered to be more FAMILY-ORIENTATED, NUDIST or GAY.

Nightlife

One of the best ways to pass an evening in Sitges is to walk the waterfront esplanade, have a leisurely DINNER, then retreat around 11 pm to one of the open-air cafes for a nightcap and some serious people-watching. If you're straight, you might have to hunt for a bay that isn't a little left of the center. There are numerous GAY BARS; in fact, there is a distributed map pinpointing them. Nine of them are concentrated on Carrae Sant Bonaventura in the center, a 5-minute walk from the beach. If you go bored with one, you have to take a few steps left or right, and you'll find the next one.

Sitges has specific areas which consist of whole clusters of bars and NIGHTCLUBS. Most people heading to Sitges for a night out will have heard of the infamous 'Street of Sin' (Carrer del Pecat') Carrer 1er de Maig. It is called this because it is lined with places to drink, dance and practice your chat-up lines! It is the home of smaller clubs such as Titos and Pacha's official bar, Pachito. It is also worth checking the smaller side streets that come off from the Street of Sin. These are full of small clubs and bars. Another famous street for bars and clubs is Carrer Santa Bonaventura. This street is the home to some smaller and, at times more strictly gay clubs, including Man.

Good To Know

✓ Address: Sitges Barcelona, Spain.

✓ Transport: By Car via C-31 or C-32 | By Train (RENFE) R2 from Passeig de Gràcia or Sants stations | By Bus MonBus from Plaza Espanya and Ronda Universitat | By Plane El Prat de Llobregat (BCN) airport or Reus/Tarragona (REU)

Wherever you stay in Barcelona, Sitges is not far for a day trip, its just a train ride away from Barcelona. You can experience all the amazing sites and activities that Sitges has to offer. Most importantly, it's a great day out with the kids, for couples or even with friends, the city is quite diverse and holds so much to do. So plan your day and come to visit Sitges!

The Beaches of Sitges

Where to swim in the city and its surroundings

The 4 kilometers long coast of SITGES comprehends 17 beaches. Another 5 beaches are found between the city and Castelldefels. Although the beaches of Sitges are all welcoming and have a laid-back atmosphere, depending on what one looks for there are some peculiarities that are characteristic of a few ones.

There are three gay-friendly beaches. The first one, Playa del Muerto, is a nudist beach on the further east side of the city. That beach is located at the bottom of a cliff and has somewhat agitated waters, which makes it hard to go in and come out of the sea. The second one is Playa de la Bassa Rodona, which is located in the heart of the city. The urban beach is the most popular among the gay community of the town, but lately has been attracting a high number of straights for the relaxing atmosphere. The Playa de la Balmins is the third gay-friendly beach of Sitges.

It also is common for the naturist practices, and even though it used to be exclusively straight, it has become mixed due to the open-mindedness of the locals

Besides the two nudists beaches mentioned above, Playa D'Aiguadolç also adopts the practices. It is fifteen minutes away from Playa de la Balmins and it also welcomes all types of crowd. At all naturist beaches, nudism is not mandatory, meaning nobody will force anybody to take off their clothes, so everybody can enjoy the beach weather they're wearing speedos or not. The most popular family beach is Playa de la Fragata. La Fragata has a small yacht club which makes a great view for walks and the sporty people who want to learn how to sailboat. Playa de Sant Sebastian is located very close to the center of the village, which makes it the most famous beach of Sitges. The 200 meters beach has its own promenade with restaurants, bars and shops that carry an exciting yet relaxing aura. The safest beach to swim with children is Playa Anquines. The man-made beach was built in the 1920's for the enjoyment of the Hotel Terramar's guests. Now a day the beach is public, and the two breakwaters at each end make it almost impossible for ocean swells to hit the sand.

For the ones who are not very keen of the salty water and sand, Poble Sec has a solution. The neighborhood of Sitges holds the city's public gym, which annexes a 500 meters swimming pool. Sitges has many options of swimming spots for all kinds of taste, which makes it a great HOLIDAY DESTINATIONto everybody.

La Fragata Beach Sitges

Overlooked by the towns beautiful whitewashed church, La Fragata Beach Sitges is ideal for young children and families. The cove allows for safe swimming and for convenience it's close to restaurants, bars and shops. To help keep the you entertained, there are volley ball nets, mini golf and peddle boats available along the shoreline.

Lifeguards are situated on this beach and there is a shower available for public use. There are no umbrellas, chairs or awnings on La Fragata Beach Sitges. Also there is a pleasant promenade with palm trees.

Dels Balmins Beach Sitges

If you're looking for a nudist area, then head to Dels Balmins Beach Sitges. This secluded cove is about a 15 minute walk, east from Sitges church.

Simply follow the coast road and you will eventually come to Dels Balmins Beach Sitges.

There is a small restaurant here, ideal for a spot of lunch or afternoon cocktail in the sun. Here you can be sure to feel comfortable whether you choose to loose your swimwear or not. It may be one of the only two nudist beaches in Sitges, but you certainly don't have to go nude if you don't wish.

As Dels Balmins Beach is a little out of town, it does tend to be fairly quiet, making it a peaceful location any time of the year. With a backdrop of mainly mountains, Dels Balmins Beach Sitges is also one of the prettiest and picturesque areas.

A beach bar offering drinks, food, and if you want you can take in the shade of the terrace. Also there's deckchairs and parasols, showers, lifeguard, and daily cleaning of the beach.

A further 15 minutes walk from this beach and you'll be at the second nudist area of D'Aiguadolç Beach

Passeig Maritim Sitges

Take a stroll in the sunshine along the waterfront promenade called Passeig Maritim Sitges. Many visitors to Sitges find themselves walking this beautiful promenade. Probably even several times during their stay and get the same enjoyment every time.

Passeig Maritim Sitges is a long paved coastal walkway which stretches the length of Sitges Town. This promenade runs along the Ribera Beach and is three kilometres in length. Therefore takes the average person about 30 minutes to walk at a slow pace.

The area is bordered by luxury villas, swimming pools, restaurants, hotels and bars. It is one of the most important seafront promenades along the Catalan Coast.

Marking the starting point, there is a statue of El Greco. While you can choose to walk, cycle, jog or use a Segway to explore this beautiful coastline. Furthermore, you'll quickly understand why so many people love this town and come back year after year.

Garraf National Park Sitges

Explore Garraf National Park Sitges and get up close to nature. Garraf National Park Sitges covers almost 13,000 hectares of protected limestone hills. Perfect for hiking or going on a bike ride. It straddles the Baix Llobregat and Alt Penedès districts. Also, Garraf itself is located in what is known as the Serralada. The mountain range to the Southwest of the Catalan coastal uplands. Due to the dry weather the park is characterised by limestone and dolomite rock landscape, canyons and valleys. However, visitors to the park will also find a lot of rosemary, strawberry bushes, dwarf palms and pines.

Wildlife

The Garraf Natural Park Sitges is even great for animal lovers as there are lots of birds to be found in the park. The dry conditions make the park a great site for typical Mediterranean species. Breeding birds include the Tawny Pipit, Black Eared Wheatear, Rock Thrush, Dartford Warbler, Sardinian Warbler, Southern Grey Shrike, Ortolan Bunting, Peregrine, Pallid Swift, Red-rumped Swallow and Crag Martin. Star of the show though goes to the pair of Bonelli's Eagle. Finally, it is home to reptiles such as vipers and lizards, and mammals such as Marten and Wild Boars.

Explore

Garraf National Park Sitges is also home to the Garraf Astronomical Observatory, perfect for those of you who love stargazing. People regularly observe the stars there and various information sessions are held during the warmer months. Garraf National Park may be reached by car, by bike or on foot. At the weekend there are many cyclists and hikers. The easiest way to get to the park from Sitges is from the commercial/industrial estate Polígono de Mas Alba. Driving through Mas Alba, going north (passing Caprabo on your right), at the last roundabout, take the second exit and between the car wash and the Llopis Garden Centre there is a dirt track to the right that takes you up into the park.

There are not many buildings in the park, the most representative are the masías (farmhouses) that were linked to agricultural activity such as Can Marcer, Mas Quadrell and Can Grau (wine) and Mas Maiol, el Carxol and Vallgrassa (goat herding).

Churches in Sitges

The city of SITGES has evidence of human presence since the 4th century. Naturally, it has a long history that is shown through its architecture and historical sites. Spain is a country that was born from the religious conflicts between Islam and Catholicism the latter taking the power after the *Reconquista* which had a major influence on the culture of its people, reflected on its architectonics.

The eldest one, *El Vinyet*, was built before 1326. It shows some Byzantine influence, seen on the image of Nuestra Señora del Vinyet Byzantine. The legend says a slave who was digging found the image and took its hand off with him. The sanctuary is located ten minutes away from the city center on the eastern part of the city. Address: Passeig del Doctor Gaietà Benaprés, 43

The second eldest one is located a bit further from the city center. Placed on the coastal hills of Parc Natural de Garraf, *Ermita de la Santissima Trinitat* had its first written evidence in 1375, when it was the home of hermits. Its current state is seen after a renovation during the 19th century. The hermit is of hard access, through a path from the main road, but its view pays off. It is said that on clear, sunny days it is possible to see the island of Mallorca, off the Spanish coast. Address: Carretera C-246a

The most famous church of Sitges, located on the beach, is *Iglesia de Sant Bartomeu I Santa Tecla*. The baroque style church was already standing during the 14th century. Its privileged location, between the BEACHES of Playa de la Fragata and Playa de San Sebastian, makes it the city's main postal card location. Address: Plaça de l'Ajuntament, 20

Not far from Sant Bartomeu I Santa Tecla is *Iglesia Sant Sebastia*. The temple was started to be built a little earlier than the 18th century but still hadn't been concluded until late 19th century. It shows signs of the Tuscan order and its paintings show a baroque influence. Address: Av. Balmins, 21

The most recent construction is the *Iglesia de Sant Joan*. Inaugurated in 1991, it takes Saint John as its patron saint and is part of the

Parochial of Sitges. Address: Plaça Sant Joan Baptista, s/n

Sitges' churches show a little bit more of the "pueblo's" history, as well as its people's culture. Located about 30 kilometers AWAY from Barcelona, the city is ideal for a DAY-TRIP during ones STAY in the Catalan Capital

Church of St Barthlomew Sitges

The Church of St Barthlomew Sitges is the towns most instantly recognisable landmarks. Thanks in part to its dramatic location. Perched on the Baluard headland and overlooking the Mediterranean sea. It is an iconic feature. Its asymmetrical silhouette, on a hill that dominates the beach. And is one of the most characteristic images of the town of Sitges.

The Church of St Barthlomew Sitges is visited by many tourists and locals every week, and makes a wonderful backdrop for postcard perfect photos. Visible all along the Passeig Maritim, its lofty presence means that locals refer to it simply as 'La Punta' or 'The Point'.

Although a church has existed since medieval times on the same site, the present building was constructed relatively recently in the 17th Century. But retains two Gothic tombs from its previous incarnation. Also boasts an impressive organ and Renaissance-era altarpiece. As Catholicism has dwindled somewhat post-Franco, the Parish Church has lost some of its civic significance. It is still the site of virtually every wedding in town though. Certainly a romantic setting to tie the knot or simply wander around wistfully.

History of Bacardi in Sitges

Bacardi is the largest spirits brand in the world that is private and family owned. It was founded 1862 in Santiago de Cuba as a rum distillery and today it owns over 200 brands and labels. Few people know that the story of Bacardi actually starts in Spain long before that.

In 1814, Facundo Bacardí Massó was born in SITGES. Son of a bricklayers' family, he emigrated to Cuba in 1830 when he was 16 years old, following his older brother. In 1844, Bacardi married Amalia Moreau, a wealthy French lady. After a few months, he opened his own mercantile shop. The couple had 6 children, whom played important roles in the history of the company. After an earthquake hit Santiago in 1852 and a cholera epidemic followed it, the family returned to SITGES to escape the poor conditions. Upon their return to Cuba, the business went bankrupt and Bacardi started attempting distilling rum. Rum was considered to be a cheap, low quality drink, and Bacardi developed a unique process with a type of yeast for fermentation, then filtering through charcoal and aging in white oak barrels, which made the final product transparent and fine, being the *first* white colored rum in the world. Mrs. Amalia spotted *bats* in the distillery one day and suggested it became the brands symbol. There were many bats that were scared away with a buzz. The fruit bats were attracted to the smell of the molasses. The bat figure was fundamental for Bacardi's brand recognition since back then most people in Cuba couldn't read or write.

When the Cuban War of Independence started, Bacardi's eldest son was arrested several times for joining the rebels. While the women of the family were exiled in Kingston, Jamaica, the company was run by Emilio's brothers Jose and Facundo. After the end of the Cuban war, today's popular drinks Daiquiri and Cuba Libre were both invented using Bacardi Rum. Under the management of Bacardi's son Facundo M. Bacardi, the company started its first international expansion opening a bottling plant in Barcelona in 1910.

Today, Sitges is home to the Casa Bacardi, a museum that tells more about the Heritage of the brand and the process. Besides that, at the museum there is a lounge bar for Bacardi's products tasting, a terrace and a bartender school.

Sitges is located 30km south of Barcelona and easily accessible by TRAIN. Casa Bacardi is located at the Plaça Ajuntament, right on the city center

Events Happening in Sitges

Sitges forms part of Catalunya and it's renowned worldwide for its Film festival as well as its Carnival. However, Sitges offers a lot more than one can think of. Sitges' artistic reputation comes forth in every event held in the beautiful city. If you're ever wondering what you can do whilst there, all of Sitges' important events have been mentioned below. In case you're coming from out of town or you're visiting specifically for one these events, don't worry about accommodation. We've got you COVERED!

January 5th Reyes Magos Parade

Melchor, Gaspar, and Baltasar go around with sweets giving them to children. A lot of people dress up as the three kings as well, some painting their faces and hands black. Kids also hand out letters to the kings or to their favourite king.

February (2019) 28th until March 6th- Carnival

The SITGES CARNIVAL is quite spectacular, baring the reputation as one of the gay capitals of Europe. Parades take place and the largest ones traditionally take place on Sunday. There's partying all throughout the event, however, having said this, the event is for everyone not just for adults. It suits every age group and activities for kids are also held.

March Sitges Vintage Car Rally

The Sitges Vintage Car Rally has grown in popularity and has become one of the highlights of the year for Barcelona and Sitges. Around 100 cars and motorbikes participate in this competition whilst onlookersexamine the cars. The people competing dress up in similar attire as that of the 1920s delighting their thousands of onlookers. The cars are categorised into two groups: (1) Epoch, which is the category for cars produced before 1920 (2) Vintage, which is the category for cars produced between 1909 and 1924.

June Corpus Christi in Sitges

Major streets are closed to traffic for approximately a day during Corpus Christi. Beautiful flowers are placed on the streets of Sitges creating a flower carpet. Volunteers sketch designs on the streets. Flowers are then laid over the designs. Afterward, on Sunday, a procession of the most Holy Sacrament is held

Also in June

GAY PRIDE SITGES:

The Gay Pride includes an open-air stage with celebrity guests and DJs. Floats and parades are held and people can also enjoy the wide variety of GAY BARS. The lively atmosphere and huge crowds make for an unforgettable night.

Noche de San Juan:

This feast is memorable because it celebrates the long-awaited Summer. For Catalans, this long day is very important and it's celebrated in every city. The concept behind this feast is that the sun reaches its highest point before beginning to drop and it symbolises fertility and wealth and therefore must be given strength. This strength is projected through bonfires and fireworks lit on beaches. Most people gather around bonfires celebrating together along with music and food. This event lasts all night.

August Fiesta Mayor de Sitges

Fiesta Mayor de Sitges is in honour of the apostle Saint Bartomeu and the virgin and protomartyr Santa Tecla. The reason for the festival lies in the patronage of the town and in the ownership of the parish of the town, which are shared by both compatriots since the 16th century. The devotion and introduction of the cult to Saint Bartholomew extended to the town, the patronage of Sitges and its temple corresponded only to Santa Tecla. A lot of different activities and events are held throughout the entire feast, along with concerts, parties, and speeches from different people.

October International Film Festival

This is the number one FILM FESTIVAL in the world. This festival stimulates a universe of encounters, exhibitions, presentations, and screenings of fantasy films from all over the world. It started in 1968 and nowadays, celebrities from all over the world travel to Sitges. Top level movie stars such as directors and producers fly out to Sitges in order to celebrate the creation of art through films.

Also in October

Wine Festival Sitges:

The best Catalan wines are presented to locals and tourists. Anyone can go and taste these magnificent wines and it's also possible to buy them. Also known as 'Festa de la Verema' or Wine Harvest Festival. This event happens in the PENEDÈS Region and there is a variety of wine tasting, food stalls, grape treading as well as barrel carrying contests which take place on Sunday. The winemaking ritual is a festival for both family and friends.

Best Bars in Sitges

The coastal town of Sitges is located 35 miles south of Barcelona and, despite its relatively small size, it is home to some great bars which offer enjoyment for a wide variety of people. True to its stereotype, the night life offering of Sitges is predominately focused on the gay community. However, the social scene in Sitges, much like the community it inhabits, it very welcoming and there are an array of bars to visit ranging from low key gin bars to vibrant themed bars. We at BARCELONA-HOME have hand picked the best bars in Sitges which we believe will provide great atmospheres and even better drinks for all who visit this beautiful town. Here is our Top five bars.

El Piano

El Piano bar is a theatrical themed bar which offers great music, including live cabaret performancesform highly entertaining professional performers. Known as one of Sitges' most popular bars, its welcoming staff and contagious atmosphere make it the perfect spot for those who like live music and performances to enjoy a drink. They also have sing-a-long video clips which encourage people to join in on the fun and sing nostalgically to much loved classic show tunes and latest hits.

Address: Sant Bonaventura, 37, 08870, sitges, Barcelona, Spain.

Opening hours: 22:30- 03:00

Varamar

Located by the picturesque beach of Sant Sebastia, Varamar is a prime location to grab a drink for both tourists and locals due to its famous cocktail menu. Their specialties, which are as picture perfect as they are tasty, include classics such as Mojitos, San Fransiscos and Pina

Coladas. They also have a strong signature cocktail game including cocktails such as Vora Vora, the Pirate and Tropics. Varamar is decorated in a nautical theme, with low lighting and dark wooden finishes and is the perfect spot to relax and enjoy a cocktail by the beach.

Address: Carrer de Port Alegre, 55, 08870, Sitges, Barcelona.

Opening hours: Monday, Tuesday and Thursday- 16:00- 01:30

Friday-Sunday- 12:00- 02:00

El Gin Tub

El Gin Tub is exactly what it says; a bar dedicated to serving an extensive selection of Gins. They create gin cocktails using homemade aromatics, infusions and bitters, meaning you can design your drink to your exact liking. The best part is that they brew their own gun on site, making it a truly unique experience. Entering this basement bar, the decor will transport you to an old Englishmen's club and even features a cast iron Victorian bathtub in the middle of the floor. The var also features live music and burlesque shows, adding to its classy and sophisticated atmosphere.

Address: Carrer de Les Parellades, 43, 08870, Sitges, Barcelona.

Opening hours: 19:00- 04:00

Bar 7 7

Ba7 7 is one of the longest running and one of the best bar in Sitges and is frequented predominately by the gay community. It is a lively bar, especially during the summer months, known for its great customer service and friendly welcome from the owners Hector and Marco. The atmosphere is light and fun, and the bar is hugely popular with with expats as it offers the opportunity to chat and drink with people form all over the globe.This lively pub hosts various events throughout the year celebrating such time as Sant Bartomeu, Santa Tecla and popular gay culture holidays such as Bears Week.

Address: Carrer Nou, 7, 08870, sitges, Barcelona.
Opening hours: 22:00- 02:30

La Sitgentana Craftbeer

La Sitgentana Craftbeer is a bar with a difference! If you have jumped on the hipster band wagon and have become a connoisseur of craft beer, or if you simply love tasting locally brewed beer, then a visit to La Sitgentana is a must. This is a bar which brews its own beer called Sitges Real Ale and the variety of its brews means that there is a beer to suit everyone's taste. Examples of their beers include: Maricel- an American pale

ale, Baluard,a London brown ale, Vinyet- a robust porter and Llucifer- a red rye IPA.

Address: Spanien, Carrer de Sant Bartomeu, 10, 08870, Sitges, Barcelona.
Opening hours: 18:30- 23:30

Best Shopping Places in Sitges

If you wish to take a break from the TANNING and sightseeing and would like to get to know a bit more from what the city has to offer to fashion, make sure you know where to go. Shopping in Sitges takes a curious pathway. There are four main shopping streets in Sitges: Carrer Sant Francesc, Carrer Parellades, Carrer Major and Carrer Jesus. The four streets end together in one point, where the Cap de la Villa is located. Besides clothing and fashion accessories stores, those streets are home to cafes, restaurants and patisseries.

SITGES is also home to several major chain stores. United Colors of Benetton, Adolfo Dominguez, Women's Secret, Le Garçon and Yamamay are some examples. But shopping in Sitges also has its unique places. Small boutiques and local stores full of personality are spread throughout the city to fulfill all wishes and tastes. Most of the big chains are located on *Carrer Sant Francesc*, the shopping street north of the *Cap de la Villa*. All others are locating on the surroundings. Stores are not only limited to those four streets, but are mostly concentrated on the area. Shops in Spain usually open from 10am until 2pm and then from 5pm until 8pm. Although local and smaller stores usually follow that schedule, for being a major touristic location, most shops especially the chain ones don't practice siesta and stay open until 9pm, mostly during the high season months.

Since Sitges is widely known for its peculiar GAY COMMUNITY, a few stores in the city are dedicated to them. Es Collection, placed on Carrer Parellades, is a famous men-clothing line and it has become quite popular for its swimwear. Menswear Sitges es4u is also quite popular for being gay-friendly.

For its dimension and urban structure, Sitges still doesn't offer a big variety of shops. In case one is looking for more *specific* shopping, Barcelona is only 30 minutes away by train, and is considered to be one of the biggest shopping cities in Europe. The Catalan Capital is home to several luxury boutiques such as Hermes, Versace, Valentino, Gucci, Chanel, Louis Vuitton and Prada. Besides the luxury boutiques, Zara is present on every corner of Barcelona. The Spanish-owned Inditex brand has accessible yet highly fashionable pieces. Also, Corte Ingles, the Spanish department store, is located on the famous shopping street. One of Barcelona's train stations is located exactly under the main shopping street, Passeig de Gracia, with incoming TRAINS from Sitges every 30 minutes.

Best Places to Visit in Catalonia

Bordered by the mountains and the Mediterranean Sea, Catalonia is a traditional region of Spain that is fiercely proud of its unique culture. Barcelona is the most-visited destination. This colorful seaside city is full of attractions and things to do, with an atmospheric medieval quarter, surprising modernist architecture, and a vibrant urban culture. Rivaling Barcelona in historic importance are

Girona, with its medieval heritage, and Tarragona, a former Roman capital.

Farther afield, in the idyllic countryside of verdant valleys and gently rolling hills, tourists can discover quaint medieval towns, picturesque seaports, and quiet country villages where chirping birds and church bells are the loudest noises. The Catalan coast delights sun-worshippers with seaside destinations such as the upscale resort of Sitges and the secluded coves of Cadaqués on the Costa Brava and the calm waters of the Costa Daurada. Every stop along the way, the local gastronomy will tempt visitors. Be sure to try local specialties like *Esqueixada,* a salad of peppers, tomatoes, and salt cod.

Barcelona

Sunny and vibrant Barcelona offers stunning Mediterranean scenery combined with bustling urban energy. This flamboyant city is Spain's second largest city as well as the capital of the Catalonia region. The Barri Gotic (Gothic Quarter) is the old town, a delightful area of impossibly narrow streets, atmospheric alleyways, and quiet squares where locals gather to socialize. Street musicians are often found here playing classical Spanish guitar, adding to the magical ambience.

Outside the old town are broad, tree-lined avenues that lead to the beautiful beaches along the harbor. Barcelona's most lively thoroughfare is La Rambla, a tree-lined street with many shops and outdoor cafés. La Rambla is at the center of the city's social life and buzzes with activity day and night. While strolling this avenue, don't miss the Palau Guell, a masterpiece of avant-garde architecture by Antoni Gaudi. Other must-see landmarks created by the celebrated architect are the Basilica de Sagrada Familia, a surreal place of spiritual worship, and the UNESCO-listed Park Guell, a fantastical park featuring whimsical benches and fountains decorated with colorful ceramic fragments.

Barcelona is famous for its culture and gourmet cuisine. The city has more than 70 top-notch museums and 24 Michelin-starred restaurants. Be sure to visit the Picasso Museum and National Museum of Catalan Art. For a delectable Catalan gastronomic experience, try one of Barcelona's finest restaurants. The two-star Michelin-rated Moments Restaurant is on the elegant Passeig de Gràcia (number 38), a few steps away from Gaudi's Casa Batlló and a few blocks from the Casa Mila, the most famous mansion designed by Gaudi.

The Costa Brava

Stretching north east from the coves and beaches of Blanes to Catalonia's border with France, the Costa Brava is Spain's most beautiful coastline. This 1,240-mile coast of ragged cliffs and idyllic beaches is one of Europe's favorite seaside playgrounds, and its pretty little whitewashed towns have lured artists that include Dali, Picasso, and Marc Chagall. Sandy beaches, like the one at the colorful old fishing village of Calella de Palafrugell, are tucked into coves beneath the cliffs, and other towns, such as Santa Susanna, have a choice of several beaches, from busy strands filled with sunbathers and kiosks to quiet coves and beaches equipped for watersports and sailing. Whatever your taste in beaches, you're sure to find it somewhere along the Costa Brava.

The Monastery of Montserrat

The beautiful Benedictine monastery of Montserrat sits atop a rocky crag, surrounded by fantastically eroded cliffs. Its history goes back to 1025, when it was founded at the site of the little mountain hermitage of Santa Maria de Montserrat. Pilgrims soon spread word of miracles performed here by the Virgin, and the monastery grew into an important place of pilgrimage. The 12th-century carving of Our Lady of Montserrat, known as La Moreneta (the Dark One), is venerated here by the faithful, and Montserrat has become one of Spain's biggest tourist attractions. The famed boys' choir, the Escolania, is one of the oldest in Europe. There is a museum of art and sacred treasures, and a funicular can take you up the mountain for sweeping views across the Catalonian countryside.

Girona

A sparkling gem of historic Catalonia 103 kilometers from Barcelona, this medieval walled city has a rich cultural heritage with diverse influences from the ancient Romans, Moorish-era Arabs, and Jews. The Old Town was built on the right bank of the Onyar River with colorful houses flanking the waterside. Girona has two areas enclosed within ancient ramparts: the Força Vella, which outlines the original Roman city founded more than 2,000 year ago, and the Medieval Quarter, which expanded the city in the 14th and 15th centuries. These atmospheric historic quarters are filled with narrow pedestrian streets and impressive medieval buildings.

The fortress-like Romanesque cathedral was built in the 11th century and updated through the 17th century. The facade is Baroque and the interior is Gothic. The massive nave is the widest medieval sanctuary in Europe. Among the artistic masterpieces displayed in the sanctuary is a Catalan textile of the Romanesque era called the Creation Tapestry. Other important religious monuments are the 12th-century Benedictine monastery de Sant Pere de Galligants; the Romanesque church of Sant Nicolau, now used as an exhibition room; and the medieval Gothic convent of Sant Doménech surrounded by beautiful gardens.

The main drag of the Old Town is the Rambla de la Libertad, an arcaded pedestrian street lined with shops and pavement cafés. Another interesting area to explore is theJewish Quarter (El Call), one of the best preserved in Spain. During the Middle Ages, this quarter had an important synagogue and centers of Kabbalist study. The squares of Placa del Oli and the Placa del Vi have maintained their original ambience.

Near the Jewish quarter, visitors can uncover the cultural legacy of the Moors. The Arab Baths, now housed in a Capuchin convent, feature a pavilion of Islamic-style columns topped with an octagonal cupola.

Tarragona

Tarragona is a beautiful seaside city that seems to have it all: sunshine, beaches, and interesting historic monuments. About 100 kilometers from Barcelona, this port town on the Costa Daurada is a worthwhile excursion or an alternative base to explore Catalonia. Beach lovers will be content spending a few days here. Most of the city overlooks the Mediterranean Sea, and the spectacular Playa del Milagro beach is within walking distance from the historic center of town. History buffs will be enthralled by Tarragona's UNESCO-listed ancient Roman buildings found all over Tarragona, especially the incredibly well-preserved Roman amphitheater of the second century. The city also has a charming Romanesque-era cathedral and medieval streets. For a delicious seafood meal, stroll over to El Serrallo - the old fishing village that has an atmospheric Old World ambience.

Sitges

Along the Mediterranean Sea, just 42 kilometers from Barcelona, Sitges lures visitors in search of golden beaches and pampered seaside relaxation. The town has a "Blue Flag" beach with calm waters ideal for swimming. A yacht marina and golf courses add to the resort ambience. Sitges also offers culture; its historic center has two lovely churches, the Iglesia de Sant Bartomeu and the Iglesia de Santa Tecla. During the late 19th and early 20th centuries, many Spanish Modernist monuments were built throughout the town. An excellent example of this avant-garde Modernist architecture is the Cau Ferrat where famous Spanish author and artist Santiago Rusiñol lived. His home and art studio became a gathering place that attracted many artists and intellectuals, giving the town a Bohemian atmosphere. For those who appreciate gourmet cuisine, Sitges has much to offer. The town has an abundance of renowned restaurants that serve superb gastronomic cuisine, especially dishes of the Catalan region.

The Salvador Dalí Theatre-Museum in Figueres

Famous for its association with Salvador Dalí, the traditional Catalan town of Figueres lies in a quiet river plain of the Girona province (140 kilometers from Barcelona). The town's main tourist attraction is the Salvador Dalí Theatre-Museum, which is devoted to the work of the Surrealist genius. Housed in the 19th-century

Municipal Theater, the museum presents all aspects of Dalí's art and displays some of his greatest masterpieces of painting. With its expansive assortment, the collection shows the artist's full range of creative expression. The museum also has a film library, which contains a collection of audiovisual content that was created by Salvador Dalí. During the month of August, the museum has nighttime openings from 10pm until 1am for a magical atmosphere that adds to the Surrealist experience. Throughout the year, the museum hosts special events and festivals.

Address: 5 Plaza Gala-Salvador Dalí, 17600 Figueres

Cadaqués and Cap de Creus Natural Park

Near the Cap de Creus Natural Park, Cadaqués is a beautiful spot on the Costa Brava coastline 170 kilometers from Barcelona. With its whitewashed houses hugging a sheltered bay, the historic quarter of Cadaqués has a distinct Mediterranean seaport ambience. The village has charmed artists for decades and still offers a vibrant cultural scene, with many art galleries and museums. Cap de Creus Natural Park has a wonderful unspoiled beach in a protected cove surrounded by pine trees, one of a number where you can swim in the crystal-clear turquoise waters along this protected strip of coast. The rugged and rocky shoreline of Cap de Creus Natural Park is also a great place for hiking and nature walks. The beautiful coastal town of Roses, nearby, began as an ancient Greek colony, and its impressive Renaissance citadel overlooks the Mediterranean Sea.

Monasterio de Santa María de Poblet

The UNESCO-listed monastery of Santa María de Poblet is 141 kilometers from Barcelona in a beautiful setting. This remarkable monument was founded in the 12th century for Cistercian monks, and the order still uses this space for their spiritual worship. Inside the monastery's church are the tombs of the Kings of Aragon. The entire monastery complex is an impressive sight surrounded by a serene landscape. The complex has two museums: the Poblet museum housed in the 14th-century Palace of King Martin that displays Romanesque, Gothic, and Baroque religious art; and the Restoration Museum that illustrates the restoration work of the monastery.

Address: Monasterio de Poblet, 43448 Vimbodi

Medieval Vic

Vic is a quaint medieval town in a peaceful setting along the banks of the Meder River, about 72 kilometers from Barcelona. The town has two historic quarters: the area around Castillo de Montcada and around the cathedral. Be sure to go inside the cathedral to admire the murals by Josep María Sert. Vic has an impressive artistic heritage, which can be further discovered at the Episcopal Museum. This museum displays masterpieces of religious painting and sculpture from the Romanesque and medieval periods. Tourists seeking a break from sightseeing should head to the Plaza Mayor for a snack at one of the cafés with a pleasant outdoor terrace. For those seeking a pampering overnight stay, the luxurious Parador Vic-Sau is the perfect choice. Surrounded by idyllic gardens, this Catalan country house was converted to an upscale hotel with an excellent gourmet restaurant.

Besalú

A picture-perfect medieval town, Besalú is a quaint jumble of cobblestone streets and quiet squares that reveal impressive historic buildings. The town has an atmospheric old Sephardic quarter with medieval Jewish baths that were used for ritual ablutions. Several fascinating ancient Christian monuments are found in Besalú including the 10th-century Benedictine monastery of Sant Pere, the 10th-century chapel of Santa María, the 13th-century Romanesque church of Sant Vicenç, and the 17th-century church of Sant Julià. Another vestige of the town's past is the Viejo Bridge built in the 11th century and renovated in the 14th century. Besalú is 133 kilometers from Barcelona in a lovely area of Catalonia, near La Garrotxa Nature Reserve in the rolling hills of the Pyrenees.

Olot and the Pyrenees Foothills

In the beautiful Pyrenees foothills (112 kilometers from Barcelona), Olot has a relaxed atmosphere and a vibrant cultural life. The town has many fascinating art galleries, and the Regional Museum boasts an excellent collection of Modernist paintings. Be sure to see the 18th-century parish church of Sant Esteve, with its marvelous Baroque altarpiece. Pleasant tree-lined avenues, quaint outdoor cafés, and old aristocratic mansions give the town an elegant ambience. Nature lovers will enjoy an excursion from Olot to the Parque Natural de la Garrotxa to discover an amazing rugged landscape formed by volcanoes.

Seu d'Urgell

Travelers can enjoy a relaxing escape to a peaceful country town in La Seu d'Urgell. It lies in a stunning natural setting with the Catalonia mountains and Andorra Pyrenees as a backdrop.

This picturesque historic town is in the Lleida province, 173 kilometers from Barcelona and 88 kilometers away from the Aigüestortes i Estany de Sant Maurici National Park. The most interesting site is the Italian-influenced Romanesque cathedral, built in the 11th and 12th centuries. Other important monuments are the 11th-century Romanesque church of Sant Miquel, the 15th-century Ayuntamiento(City Hall) and the convent of Sant Domingo that has been converted into a Parador de Turismo hotel.

The Romanesque Monastery of Santa María de Ripoll

This magnificent Romanesque monastery was an important monastic center in Catalonia during the Middle Ages. Dating from the 12th century, the complex includes a church with an extraordinary portico depicting biblical scenes and a peaceful cloister designed to inspire spiritual contemplation. Another noteworthy religious monument of Ripoll is the 12th-century Iglesia de Sant Pere featuring pre-Romanesque architectural elements. The church now houses the town's ethnographic museum. In the 19th century with the arrival of the railway, Ripoll became a bustling commercial town with a booming textile industry. Ripoll lies 109 kilometers from Barcelona.

Banyoles

This idyllic retreat in nature is just 18 kilometers from Girona and 121 kilometers from Barcelona, near La Garrotxa Nature Reserve. Surrounded by the green rolling hills of the Sierra Rocacorba, the town is nestled between two rivers on the shores of Lake Banyoles. Banyoles has an ancient history, with an important textile industry since the 13th century. In the town's quaint old center are several interesting religious monuments: the

14th-century church of Santa María del Turers and the Neoclassical monastery of Sant Esteve. Other important landmarks are the Pia Almoina, a medieval mansion built in the 14th century that houses an Archaeology Museum,and the Llotja del Tint, a 15th-century building that was used for dyeing textiles. A highlight of visiting Banyoles is the beautiful lake with a six-kilometer perimeter. It's a wonderful place to relax, take nature walks, cycle, or go boating. Tourists may rent small boats for rowing, kayaking, or canoeing. Fishing is another popular pastime, with rewarding catches to be found in the pristine waters.

Cathedral of Solsona

The splendid Cathedral of Solsona, 107 kilometers from Barcelona, was built in the 14th century in Gothic style but reveals the architectural elements of an earlier Romanesque church. Typical of Romanesque style, the interior has three apses decorated with arcades. The bell tower is also from the original Romanesque structure. Visitors are surprised by the spacious single-nave vaulted interior. The facade features Baroque adornment added in the 18th century, and the Neoclassical cloister displays a Romanesque stone icon of the Virgin of the Cloister.

Embalse de Talarn

About eight kilometers to the north of Tremp is the Embalse de Talarn, a large lake formed by a dam that supplies a hydroelectric station. One of the largest bodies of freshwater in Catalonia, the lake is surrounded by beautiful scenery, with many pine trees and secluded coves. Fishing, bird watching, boating, sailing, and camping are all popular things to do here, and sign-posted hiking and 4x4 trails also weave through the rugged train.

Five Best Day Trips From Sitges

Portaventure Theme Park

Less than one hour's drive from Sitges is the ever popular and children's favourite PortAventura theme park. Spread out over 296 acres are high speed thrill rides and a host of exciting attractions that chug along at a gentler pace. The park is divided into six different themed worlds. Thrill to some rootin' tootin' fun in an authentic Wild West town in the Far West.

ake younger children to SésamoAventura for the Sesame Street characters and amusements. Explore Polynesia, a jungle-like environment with rides and attractions. The other themed worlds are Mediterrània, China and Mexico.

If white knuckle adventures are your thing, PortAventura theme park has a couple of wild rollercoasters. The Shambhala has a gravity-defying fall of 78 meters, while the Furius Baco reaches a phenomenal speed of 135 kilometres per hour in three seconds. Visitors can also enjoy water-based rides, live shows and seasonal events such as the spooky activities during the Halloween period.

PortAventura is an easy 1 hour drive south from Sitges and it is motorway for most of the way. Look for signpost to the park once you pass the exit for Reus airport just south of Tarragona. There is plenty of parking at the site but note that this is charged for in addition to your park entry ticket.

Aqualeon Water Park And Zoo

There's an ocean of fun for all the family at AquaLeon Water Park and Zoo. It is two parks in one spread out over 800,000m2. Visitors can get wild and wet in the aqua park which features water slides, tubes, a rapid river and wave pool.

For those who like their aquatic adventures to come with a generous dollop of excitement, there's Toboloko, a long and very fast water rollercoaster that has a drop of 13 meters. Young children have their own water wonderland, with mini slides, a climbing frame island, pool and sprays.

Inside the animal park, more than 600 exotic creatures roam freely over close approximations to their natural habitats. Among the animals you can see are lions, llamas, brown bars and tigers. A great way to see the animals is on board the double decker safari bus that travels through the park. Young children will love spending their time in the mini zoo where they can see emus, chimpanzees and miniature horses.

Barcelona

Barcelona is one of Europe's most sophisticated, cultured and beautiful cities. Whether you enjoy the buzz of a vibrant metropolis, art, architecture, festivals and music, Barcelona has it covered.

Among the must-see attractions are the architectural splendours of one of Barcelona's most famous sons, the architect Antoni Gaudi. They include the Basilica de la Sagrada Família that looks like it's been made of dripping candle Wax, La Pedera building and Park Güell. Among the intriguing sights at this large public space are Gaudí's mosaic work on the main terrace, the serpentine bench and the colonnaded footpath.

Art lovers shouldn't miss the Picasso Museum that displays the master's early sketches and Blue Period works. Go on a walking tour of the Gothic Quarter and treat the children to some science fun at Barcelona's Natural Sciences Museum. Amble along the tree-lined pedestrian thoroughfare known as La Rambla. Browse its shops and enjoy some tapas in a bar or restaurant.

Top up the tan by heading out to the city's beaches and meander along the beachfront promenade. For a different perspective on things take the cable car to Montjuïc Mountain. Round off the day with a concert at Gran Teatre del Liceu or at L'Auditori.

For many people this city is the home of one of the world's greatest football clubs - FC Barcelona. It is relatively easy to get tickets for FC Barcelona home matches, however, if there are no matches on while you are there you can still experience the excitement and magic of the Camp Nou with the official Camp Nou Experience Tour & Museum. This is a great day out for any football fan.

 The city is less than an hour's drive away from Sitges and there are also regular and cheap buses and trains from the town.

The Garraf Natural Park

The Garraf Natural Park surrounds the town of Sitges and provides a fantastic resource for nature lovers, sports enthusiats and those that appreciate wide open natural spaces. Natural lovers can get out and explore the geology, flora and fauna of Garraf Nature Park. The vast area covers 12,820 hectares and encompasses woodland areas of holm oak and white pine, closed valleys and regions of limestone and dolomite rocks.

There are numerous signposted trekking routes through the park which can be traversed on your own or with an expert guide. At the heart of the park is the Palau Novella, where you'll find Catalonia's first Buddhist monastery. Among the wildlife that you may see in the park are Mediterranean tortoises, rabbits, quails, wild boar, eagles and falcons. Many of our villas are located right on the doorstep of the Garraf Natural Park providing easy access to hundreds of kilometres of excellent walking and mountain bike trails.

Penedes Wine And Cava Region

Wine lovers who visit Sitges have much to look forward to with the town's close proximity to the Penedes Wine Region, home to mile upon mile of vineyards and a countryside dotted with museums, towns and farmhouses.

Embark on tours of some of the vineyards and wineries such as Torres Winery and Bodegues Sumarroca.Venture into cellars to taste wines, and in some places cava. Perhaps even go on a wine tasting course. Penedes Wine Region also features numerous attractions that are well worth putting on the travel itinerary.

See vintage train carriages at the Catalonia Railway Museum. Sample fine chocolates at the Simón Coll Chocolate Experience. Discover more of the area by trekking through its nature routes and visiting its nature parks. At Les Deus Adventure Park you can try zip-line rides above trees and rocky landscapes.

There's also a lot of fascinating history to explore in some of the region's castles. They include Mediaeval Castle of Calafell and Gelida Castle.

Heritage

Sitges is a city fully dedicated to arts. Since the appearance of the "Escola Lluminista" (Illuminist School) during the middle of the nineteenth century –that included a number of artists captivated by the light of Sitgesthe population transformed culture in one of its main identifying features. Sitges became a destination for artists, writers and other artists who have helped to draw a human landscape sensitive to the arts and participate in its creation. And while the stage for a long list of cultural events from different disciplines; the town is also in permanent artistic ferment. Festivals, cultural tours, cultural performances and a wide ranging cultural and social fabric, transforms the agenda of the town in a permanent dynamic movement.

Sitges has a rich legacy not only in museums, but also in buildings or residential areas. The Parish Church of Sant Bartomeu i Santa Tecla -the most famous landscape of Sitges- dates from the seventeenth century, and inside there are various baroque altarpieces of remarkable artistic and cultural value as well as a beautiful organ dating from 1699 and recently restored.

The old town of Sitges includes other buildings that are amply recognized. The ensemble of Maricel, also including the Palace and the Museum, houses the Historical Archive of Sitges and the Santiago Rusiñol Library, which contains a known library specializing in artistic and literary movements of the late nineteenth and early twentieth century's, and also the collections Rusiñol and Miquel Utrillo.

The Town Hall is next and occupies the space of the Castle of Sitges, the new building was built by Salvador Vinyals in 1889 to house the town hall. The Old Market , a modernist building built by Gaietà Buïgas the same year, now housing Casa Bacardi. In the fifties of the twentieth century, the Fish Market was built as an attachment, since 2011 the headquarters of Fundació Stämpfli.

The list of unique buildings of the town is significant and fills the streets of Sitges and much of the seafront. The homes of "Americanos", the people from Sitges who returned from Cuba after the nineteenth century with small fortunes who built up one of the urban aspects of Sitges, such houses live alongside lavish mansions from the early twentieth century located in the

Promenade of the Terramar community, a "Noucentista" city-garden that stood at the forefront of residential tourism.

The medieval city walls, the Palace of the Moorish King (19th Century), the Chapel of Vinyet (1773), the Chapel of Sant Sebastian (1861), the Buildings of Casino Prado and the Hospital of Sant Joan Baptista (1910), the former slaughterhouse (1925), or the gardens of Terramar are other buildings in the town.

Sitges hosts outstanding cultural events. The Sitges - International Fantastic Film Festival of Catalonia, founded in 1968, is the most important and relevant and considered the greatest fantasy film festival in the world. Other festivals hosted by Sitges are Jazz Antic Sitges, the Week Catalonia - America, the Summer Concert Series (created in 1976), the

International Tango Festival, or the Irish Catalan Festival - Creative Connections, among others. The Art Fair, the exhibition of different art galleries and the stable schedule of the Department of Culture, as well as the activities of the Cercle Artistic de Sitges are other important cultural events.

The End